GOD'S ORDER
and
PURPOSE
of
MARRIAGE

Samuel Kioko Kiema

ISBN 978-1-953223-16-6 (paperback)
ISBN 978-1-953223-21-0 (digital)

Copyright © 2020 by Samuel Kioko Kiema

All rights reserved. No part of this publication may be reproduced, distributed, or transmitted in any form or by any means, including photocopying, recording, or other electronic or mechanical methods without the prior written permission of the publisher. For permission requests, solicit the publisher via the address below.

Rushmore Press LLC
1 800 460 9188
www.rushmorepress.com

Printed in the United States of America

Acknowledgments

First, to my Lord and Savior, Jesus Christ, who has prepared and anointed me to herald His gospel. I am honored to be charged with such a responsibility. I am forever grateful for His perpetual grace upon my life so that I may make known the power of His gospel. Thank You, Lord, for delighting in the prosperity of Your servant. I declare my best days are with me, speaking blessing, favor, increase, and multiplication into my tomorrow.

To my beautiful, excellent, godly wife; my intimate and covenant friend; the love of my life; and my coworker in God's purpose, Jedidah, who continues to show me the joy of life. I thank the Lord for such a perfect match for my strengths and weaknesses. The trust you have in my ability to see and hear from God causes me to walk in a deeper level of fear of the Lord. I thank you for your chaste conduct accompanied with godly fear and for sharing this work with me and encouraging me to do all that God has assigned us. You are the most profound representation of Jesus I have ever known. Your walk of love, humility, forgiveness, gentleness, and faith challenge me daily. I thank you for being a loving mother to our three children, Faith, Susan, and Samuel Jr., whom you have helped to raise in the fear of the Lord. I thank you for believing the gift of God in me and requesting that I write this book. What a treasure and jewel you are to me. You are my world, my sunshine, my precious gift from the Father. Through you I have obtained favor with the Lord. Thank you for trusting me to lead you into the purposes of God. My world revolves around you.

To my bishop, apostle, and prophetic friend, Bishop Clarence E. McClendon of Full Harvest International Church and of Clarence

E. McClendon Ministries, who helped father me into the service of our Lord Jesus Christ to connect people to the power of God. Thank you for prophesying to my destiny, preaching revelatory rhema word, teaching, and training me how to speak God's Word to situations that speak contrary to my destiny, how to pray the word of God and get results, how to hear the voice of God, and how to discern and respond to issues knowing that the issue is never the issue in the situation. You helped develop the gifts of God in me. I honor you.

To my mother, Martha, who helped raise me in the fear of God amid destitution and impoverishment and believed that I would become a blessing, knowing that I was called to this and would become a blessing to others. I am blessed by your strength and your example of humility. You discerned the gift of God in me and helped to develop it. I call you blessed.

To the faithful, trustworthy covenant friend pastor Josephine Kanywele, whom the Lord has connected to the anointing that is in resident in our life as we seek to connect people to the kingdom of God and equip the saints for the work of the ministry, establishing them in the foundation of God that stands sure. Thank you for encouraging my faith and strengthening me in the things of God by sowing into the anointing for the *Great Commission* to prepare people to enter into the kingdom of our Lord. May the Lord give you increase more and more, you and your children. I call you coworker with us in the Lord's big business.

To daughters, Faith-Kiema Phillips and Susan Kiema Adams, my son, Samuel Kioko Kiema Jr., my sons in-law, Seilas Phillips and Michael Adams; and my grandchildren, Solomon, Zoe, Drusilla, and Zion. I thank you for your support and maturity in releasing me to fulfill the great call in my life. The Lord bless you on credit as you mature in the things of God. You are my earthly inheritance.

Preface

Ecclesiastes 9:9-12 "⁹ Live joyfully with the wife whom you love all the days of your vain life which He has given you under the sun, all your days of vanity; for that is your portion in life, and in the labor which you perform under the sun. ¹⁰ Whatever your hand finds to do, do it with your might for there is no work or device or knowledge or wisdom in the grave where you are going. ¹¹ I returned and saw under the sun that—The race is not to the swift, Nor the battle to the strong, Nor bread to the wise, Nor riches to men of understanding, Nor favor to men of skill; But time and chance happen to them all. ¹² For man also does not know his time: Like fish taken in a cruel net, Like birds caught in a snare, so the sons of men are snared in an evil time, When it falls suddenly upon them."

Our arch enemy, the devil thrives on our ignorance. Many issues in our marriage relationship which never occurred to us as anything significant are from our ancestral bloodline. They are the snare keeping us in bondage, although we are born again.

Prayer

Father I thank you for the revelation on Your Order and purpose of marriage, and family life to communicate most desired and desperately needed wisdom, understanding, and knowledge in this most misconstrued, misunderstood and abused relationship.

As we write this gospel truth of Your kingdom, may it bring redemption, restoration and emancipation to the family unit and may You establish Your **kingdom** in their lives that Your **Will** may be done by ruling over their affairs.

We declare, vow, and decree that by Your authority the life and the light of the gospel of the kingdom shines abroad in their lives.

May Your Word be like a HAMMER and like FIRE smashing, demolishing, destroying and consuming the works of the adversary and construct what You desire in their lives. Devil quit. Stop opposing God's redeemed. We testify to you that The Father has opened the portals of heaven, great and effective doors of opportunity as they work His system. We declare to you devil, God's redeemed are armed with the sword of the spirit, which is the word of God and you should consider them dangerous. Devil, in the name of Jesus The Christ of Nazareth, we cancel your contracts, destroy ancestral familiar altars, high places of devil worship, witchcraft, sorcery, and divination are rendered powerless and have no effect in the affairs of the redeemed of the Lord. By the reason of the anointing we inflict defeat on religious dogma, doctrines and man's traditions that make the word of God of no effect. We decree destruction on plans and schemes of theft, robbery, death and destruction. Now Father, as your inheritance we submit the relationships and marriages of Your redeemed to Your authority. Father we ask You to give them everything that pertains to life and godliness. In Jesus name, So be it, Amen.

Introduction

We write this book with an open mind unto God and beseech our readers also to read it with an open mind, so you can understand and receive God's Will, Mind, and Purpose concerning your marriage. Our goal is to help marriages grow through dedicated and practical teachings from the word of God. We purpose to help husbands and wives thrive in their marriage by providing empowering knowledge to nourish and cherish each other in a healthy marriage relationship. We believe the Spirit of God has disclosed to us the mind of God relative to the reason why He created the first couple was to come into agreement to bring forth His **Kingdom**, create His **Will** on the earth as it is in heaven and become God's model on the earth. Husbands and wives, and anybody who is or plans to be in marriage relationship please understand that The Father desires for you to reflect His order, purpose, blessing, and dominion in the earth. He wants your relationship in the earth to reflect the image and model of the relationship The Father has with The Son and the image of the relationship Christ has with His church (bride). The Father's desire for you is to be like the first family He instituted in the dispensation of innocence. They believed by speaking God's Word and created hence brought forth the Father's kingdom and will on earth. We are writing this book based on the revelation of the Lord to His servant in this important matter that has been most misconstrued, mispresented, misrepresented, misapplied and has brought confusion throughout generations since the fall of mankind.

We warn you some part of our writing might be provocative and revolutionary presentation based on your definition of relationship, sex, and marriage. This book will challenge both the cultural and ecclesiastical norms and confront them with raw biblical truth. You may want to read the totality of the book because if you don't you may have imbalanced perspective on the matter.

Chapter 1

Marriage Definition

Understanding God's purpose for marriage is of the utmost importance, because to marry and miss it, is to enter a life full of frustration and disappointment setting the stage for great marital unrest and destruction of one's life.

Let us look at God's definition of marriage so we can have a crystal clear godly understanding of the picture of marriage God has in His mind, so we can draw from it.

Creator's Perspective

Marriage is union between a male man and a female man to establish a familial bond that is recognized by God, granting them mutual conjugal rights and responsibilities to accomplish His plan on earth.

Marriage is a sacred vow between male and female in a holy matrimony who understand that their union is a plan of God for their destiny to create, make, and bring forth the purpose of the coming of God's kingdom and His Will being done on earth as it is in heaven. **Matthew 6:10 KJV – "Thy kingdom come . Thy will be done in earth, as it is in heaven."**

God Started Marriage Institution

God started marriage institution from the beginning. He instituted it in the **dispensation of innocence** and is therefore a holy institution. God does not extend marriage relationship to same gender (male to male or female to female) union. Same gender marriage is hateful, detestable, obscene, indecent, immoral, abominable and demonic in the eyes of the Creator. It is a kind that is a sickening disgust, most despotic, and most unrequited fetter. From a biblical perspective, however, a proper name for "same-gender marriage" is "legalized homosexuality." Therefore, God created a marriage, a family in His own image. The identity of Family is in God.

Ephesians 3:14-15 – "For this cause I bow my knees unto the Father of our Lord Jesus Christ, of whom the whole family in heaven and earth is named".

The Identity, life, and marriage is from God. The name **family** belongs to God, and He extends it to the union of male and female only. God began marriage institution during creation and gave man (male and female) **Dominion** on earth purposely to accomplish on the earth what He has accomplished in heaven. He wanted two people on earth to agree on His **word,** so He can do on earth what has been done in heaven *Matthew 18:19 – "Again I say unto you, that if two of you shall agree on earth as touching anything that they shall ask , it shall be done for them of my Father which is in heaven".*

The union of male and female who **God joins** are the only one who can be in perfect union and agreement for the Father in heaven to do anything for them that they ask. God wanted man (male and female) to be on earth what He (Father, Son, and the Holy Spirit) is in heaven. He wanted man to be where he is what God is where He is.

Chapter 2

Purpose for Marriage

Our attitude towards marriage relationship from God's point of view should be; "What do **I Bring or Sow** into the marriage relationship rather than what do **I Get** or how do **I Benefit** from the marriage relationship." God's seed principle of prosperity is **Sowing and Reaping.** You cannot reap without sowing. You must sow the Word of God, acts of love and intercession into your marriage relationship to reap its benefits. The Bible offers guidance for married couples, husbands, wives, newlyweds, engaged and those who are desiring to find their soul mates. **Ephesians 5:23-33** describes marriage in relation to God, Jesus Christ, and the Christian faith. We shall discuss this farther under the topic of marriage models momentarily.

Mark 10:1-9 "Then He arose from there and came to the region of Judea by the other side of the Jordan. And multitudes gathered to Him again, and as He was accustomed, He taught them again. ² The Pharisees came and asked Him, "Is it lawful for a man to divorce his wife?" testing Him. ³ And He answered and said to them, "What did Moses command you?"⁴ They said, "Moses permitted a man to write a certificate of divorce, and to dismiss her." ⁵ And Jesus answered and said to them, "Because of the hardness of your heart he wrote you this precept. ⁶ But from the beginning of the creation, God 'made them male and female.' ⁷ 'For this reason a man shall leave his father and mother and be joined to his wife,⁸ and the two shall become one flesh'; so then they are no longer two, but one flesh. ⁹Therefore what God has joined together, let not man separate."

The gospel according to writer Mark quoted above speaks of relationships as God intended from the beginning. If you want to know God's way of doing things for yourself, you must go back to the beginning and find out what God said initially so you can do it His way. But the church has given the civil authority the power to define what marriage is and has abdicated its role in truly defining and understanding it spiritually and the world system and the civil authority has taken the definition beyond the biblical definition. Now the church has little recourse to fight the world's system definition because the church abdicated its right to define marriage honestly, spiritually and not merely civilly.

What we are dealing with now in our generation is a situation where both the culture and likewise the church has it wrong. They have accepted religious and traditional interpretation of relationship, sex and marriage rather than biblical articulation. What we are going to share is not the popular current cultural perspective nor the traditional religious application, but the truth the bible articulates. By reading the whole book you will have counter balance perspective biblical articulation of the word of God with revelation knowledge. We will in church say this though, no matter what condition you find yourself in and where you are there is help and hope. The word of God is never brought to condemn, it is brought to raise the biblical standard and challenge you by the power of the Holy Spirit to aspire to it. So whatever kind of relationship you are in: you are married, single or divorced; whether you are in relationship of Adam and Eve, or Adam and Steve, or Eve and Evelyn. We got to deal with this real situation because it is part of the problem. God's prophets have been silenced and religion has given inadequated and unbiblical perspective on the truth. We now have a world that is confused and a church that doesn't know what to say about marriage. However, we are not without answer, hallelujah. The word of God is the answer to everything every time, any time and all the time. We got to believe in the word of God and look at what it says and not impose what we want on what it says.

Mark 10:5 "......Because of the hardness of your heart he wrote you this precept" is a phrase that has been misunderstood and misconstrued. We shall deal with it later but permit me allude to it here. It doesn't mean that everybody who gets divorce has hardness of heart or somehow is offended.

In this verse, Jesus is approached about the subject of Divorce. Those who were asking were not asking because they wanted to know the truth, but they were looking to do something that they wanted Him to back them up. People come to God not because they want to know the truth, but because they want God to endorse, backup or support their decision. Jesus refuses to take the trap and simply says, if you want to understand anything about relationships, if you really want to know God's idea of what is proper and improper, if you want to understand about anything God has blessed and will prosper you must go back to the very beginning.

Reason for Leaving Father and Mother

Marriage is not the reason to leave father and mother's house like religion has imposed on it. The reason to leave father and mother's house is for what God did in the beginning. Mark 10:**6 "... But from the beginning of the creation, God 'made them male and female".** Compare with **"Genesis 1:27 So God created man in His *own* image; in the image of God He created him; male and female He created them and Genesis 5:2 He created them male and female, and blessed them and called them Mankind in the day they were created."**

To really know God's idea of what is proper and improper, what He has blessed and will prosper you must go back to the very beginning. You cannot start from your situation, what you beheld in class, read in school or books you read in your house written by unregenerate minds. If you want God's idea you got to go back to the beginning and see what God did and said and unwrap it from cultural, distortion and religious mythology. Jesus says if you are to understand anything about marriage, divorce or any matters pertaining to divine perspective which includes fornication, adultery, same gender unions, homosexuality, and lesbianism you got to go back to the beginning.

People can live the way they want. My job is not to try to change how they live! My job is to give divine perspective on what God says, and you choose to set before yourself death and life. We must deal with this consequential weighty matter, so we can love people who agree with us and those who disagree with us. Do you give a response to people who ask you about these things? Are you interested in God's idea or do you not care? You must have something to say about why you believe the word of God is the answer.

Chapter 3

Man Is to Be on Earth What God Is in Heaven

Let us qualify these words very quickly because they are going to be very important as you read on. The old testament is written in Hebrew language and the New testament is written in Greek which are more colorful than English language.

The Hebrew word for **Image** is **Tselem** meaning resemblance. The Hebrew word for **likeness** is **Dmuth** meaning similitude or model or similar.

Genesis 1:26-31A [26] Then God said, "Let Us make **Man** in Our image, according to Our likeness; let **Them** have dominion over the fish of the sea, over the birds of the air, and over the cattle, over all the earth and over every creeping thing that creeps on the earth." [27] So God created Man in His *own* image; in the image of God He created **Him; Male** and **Female** He created **Them.** [28] Then God blessed **Them,** and God said to **Them,** "Be fruitful and multiply; fill the earth and subdue it; have dominion over the fish of the sea, over the birds of the air, and over every living thing that moves on the earth." [29] And God said, "See, I have given you every herb *that* yields seed which *is* on the face of all the earth, and every tree whose fruit yields seed; to you it shall be for food. [30] Also, to every beast of the earth, to every bird of the air, and to everything that creeps on the earth, in which *there is* life, *I have given* every green herb for food"; and it was so. ³¹ Then God saw everything that He had made, and indeed *it was* very good.

God is both Male and Female

So, God says let us make man(Single) to resemble us in the earth and let him (Single) function in the similar analogous equivalent and comparable way we function. Let them(Plural) be our model and representative on earth. Now we know this about God, that God is both male and female. This is true because man is created in God's image, and God created man both male and female. God has both masculine element and He has feminine element or else He could not produce both. You cannot produce what you are not.

Life in God's Garden

The bible gives us the godly life we are to model on earth. We see this in Genesis 2:8-9, 15-25 **⁸ The LORD God planted a garden eastward in Eden, and there He put the man (male and female - emphasis) whom He had formed. ⁹ And out of the ground the LORD God made every tree grow that is pleasant to the sight and good for food. The tree of life was also in the midst of the garden, and the tree of the knowledge of good and evil.**

¹⁵ Then the LORD God took the man and put him in the garden of Eden to tend and keep it. ¹⁶ And the LORD God commanded the man (male and female – emphasis), saying, "Of every tree of the garden you may freely eat; ¹⁷ but of the tree of the knowledge of good and evil you shall not eat, for in the day that you eat of it you shall surely die." ¹⁸ And the LORD God said, "It is not good that man should be alone; I will make him a helper comparable to him." ¹⁹ Out of the ground the LORD God formed every beast of the field and every bird of the air, and brought them to Adam to see what he would call them. And whatever Adam called each living creature, that was its name. ²⁰ So Adam gave names to all cattle, to the birds of the air, and to every beast of the field. But

GOD'S ORDER AND PURPOSE OF MARRIAGE

for Adam there was not found a helper comparable to him. ²¹ And the L ORD God caused a deep sleep to fall on Adam, and he slept; and He took one of his ribs, and closed up the flesh in its place. ²² Then the rib which the L ORD God had taken from man He made into a woman, and He brought her to the man. ²³ And Adam said: "This is now bone of my bones and flesh of my flesh; She shall be called Woman Because she was taken out of Man." ²⁴ Therefore a man shall leave his father and mother and be joined to his wife, and they shall become one flesh. ²⁵ And they were both naked, the man and his wife, and were not ashamed".

Genesis 1:26 - Then **God** *(singular)* said, "**Let Us** *(Plural)* make man *(singular)* in **Our** *(plural)* image, according to Our *(Plural)* likeness; let them *(Plural)* have **dominion** over the fish of the sea, over the birds of the air, and over the cattle, over all[a] the earth and over every creeping thing that creeps on the earth

The phrase – **"Image of God"** is the cornerstone of the **biblical** understanding of **man/Human being.** Man is like God spiritually. That means Man has God's Character, Nature and Authority.

John 4:24 says God is Spirit and according to ***Proverbs 20:27* and *1 Corinthians 2:11-16*** Man is spirit.

John 4:24 reads: "²⁴God is Spirit, and those who worship Him must worship in spirit and truth."

"Proverbs 20:27 reads - *The spirit of a man is the lamp of the L ORD, Searching all the inner depths of his heart) and (1 Corinthians 2:11-16 ¹¹ For what man knows the things of a man except the spirit of the man which is in him? Even so no one knows the things of God except the Spirit of God. ¹² Now we have received, not the spirit of the world, but the Spirit who is from God, that we might know the things that have been freely given to us by God. ¹³ These things we also speak, not in words which man's wisdom teaches but which the Holy[a] Spirit teaches, comparing spiritual things with*

spiritual. *¹⁴ But the natural man does not receive the things of the Spirit of God, for they are foolishness to him; nor can he know them, because they are spiritually discerned. ¹⁵ But he who is spiritual judges all things, yet he himself is rightly judged by no one. ¹⁶ For "who has known the mind of the* LORD *that he may instruct Him? But we have the mind of Christ."*

Image of God is in relation to a unique social or community concept of God.

Genesis 1:27 –" So God created man in His own image; in the image of God He created him; male and female He created them".

God created man as male and female in His own image. God did not create a solitary individual, but two people in one.

"Genesis 5:1-2 …... In the day that God created man, He made him in the likeness of God. ²He created them male and female, and blessed them and called them Mankind in the day they were created"

Matthew 19:4-6 ⁴……, "Have you not read that He who made[a] *them at the beginning 'made them male and female, ⁵and said, 'For this reason a man shall leave his father and mother and be joined to his wife, and the two shall become one flesh? ⁶So then, they are no longer two but one flesh. Therefore, what God has joined together, let not man separate."* The community that reflects God's image is the special community of a male and female. This is exemplified by the following comparison between man and the creator (God)

In Genesis 2:23 And Adam said: **"This *is* now bone of my bones and flesh of my flesh; She shall be called Woman, because she was taken out of Man.".**

She is not a woman because she is a man with a womb, but because she is the man from the womb of the man (male and female). She was taken from the man (male and female) not because she has a womb. She is the female man taken out of the man (male and female). What was the reason of the female being taken out of the man and not the male man?

Chapter 4

For This Reason

Genesis 2:24 "Therefore a man shall leave his father and mother and be joined to his wife, and they shall become one flesh".

The Reason for Leaving his Father and Mother

The reason the male man shall leave his father and mother and be joined to his wife, the female man is because the female was taken out of the man (male and female). He must disconnect himself from all other relationships go and find his better half (other part) of his so he can be complete to accomplish everything God has purposed for them. God set the example man is to follow. He separates the seed from the male and joins it to the female's egg forming another man in the likeness of God. He then separates the new man child from the mother by cutting off the umbilical cord. Psalm 139:13-16 – "For You formed my inward parts; You covered me in my mother's womb. [14] I will praise You, for I am fearfully *and* wonderfully made; Marvelous are Your works, And *that* my soul knows very well. [15] My frame was not hidden from You, when I was made in secret, *And* skillfully wrought in the lowest parts of the earth. [16] Your eyes saw my substance, being yet unformed. And in Your book, they all were written, The days fashioned for me, when *as yet there were* none of them."

What we call man and woman today, God calls them male and female, husband and wife not man and wife or man and woman. There is only one man, the man, male and female. Together male and female make one individual called man in the creator's terms. That means: Male + Female = Man- (Mankind). It is erroneous to refer to the male part of the man as the man. The wife is not the chick you meet and do the deed with. She is not the woman you are attracting. There should be more than the deed and the attracting. She is the female man possessing the other half of the blessing without which the creator's purpose will not be fulfilled on earth. She is special to the Father and He will avenge her speedily if not treated right.

The Blessing and Dominion

God creates male and female and He blesses them in Genesis chapter one, but He does not take the female out of the man (male and female) until Genesis chapter two. In Genesis chapter one, both the male and female were inside the man, but He does not take the female out of the man until Genesis chapter two. In Genesis chapter one, there are no two bodies standing before God but one body standing before Him. The male is in the man and the female is in the man and God that gives life to the dead and calls those things that are not as though they were saw them in Him. Therefore, when God creates man in His image and likeness male and female He created them. "Them is not him." If then He blesses them and takes her out of him (male and female) then she has a part of that blessing and he has a part of the blessing. The blessing is incomplete until God Himself joins them together. The blessing is not what God had intended it to be until God joins the male and female to become husband and wife. God intended the blessing to be unified. God says He must keep the blessing in the earth. He must keep the blessing the way He created it. He intended the blessing to function together.

The reason is to have a complete blessing. The reason the man (both male and female) shall leave his father and mother is to complete the blessing as God intended from the beginning. Therefore, the complete blessing is the reason the man (male and female) shall leave father and mother and the husband be joined to his wife. To precisely get the complete blessing the creator urges both the male man and the female man each to leave their father and mother and He would join them together as husband and wife. The blessing is between the two joined together by God. It follows that if God does not join them he cannot bless that union. **The reason is the recreation of man (male and female).** To every union God blesses, man (male and female) is recreated. Every time God unites a male man to a female man, in a holy matrimony He blesses that union and the original intention of Elohim (Eternal Creator) is created. That is why Jesus attends every wedding to which He is invited to oversee the creation. The first miracle Jesus performed was of the wedding of Canna of Galilee where he was invited. The reason for the invite was to oversee the creation of the man (male and female) He created and blessed the union. At this point I am impressed of the Holy Spirit to challenge husbands and wives both alike to invite Jesus in your union regardless of how you were joined together, whether through rebellion, disobedience, ignorance, eloping, rape, force, men's traditions, arranged marriage etc., you are not getting what you deserve. Non, of us (Christians) is getting what we deserve because we all have sinned and fall short of God's goodness. His grace is sufficient to forgive, recreate and bless the union to the original intention of Elohim if we invite Him to perform the wedding. If you are born again the bible in Romans 8:1 says, **"there is therefore now no condemnation to them which are in Christ Jesus, who walk not after the flesh, but after the Spirit."** How God accepts you is not by your past performance, but by His grace apart from you having worked for it. You are right with God through the work that Christ accomplished without your performing for it. It doesn't matter your economic status, ethnicity, gender, or color the gospel is the equalizer. The gospel gives the same access to all. The bible points this out and says in **Romans**

3:23-26 "for all have sinned and fall short of the glory of God, being justified freely by His grace through the redemption that is in Christ Jesus, whom God set forth *as* a propitiation by His blood, through faith, to demonstrate His righteousness, because in His forbearance God had passed over the sins that were previously committed, to demonstrate at the present time His righteousness, that He might be just and the justifier of the one who has faith in Jesus." No matter how good I am, how good I try to be, how excellent my day is, (not me but the deed) still falls short of the glory of God but we have been justified. Your marriage that is not working is in the past being justified freely by His grace. Our justification in Christ is what makes our righteousness before God a reality, but so many Christians are afraid to live in the liberty of this free acceptance by God. When you agree with the word of God and do it you have the right standing with God which He supplies through faith in Jesus Christ.

While God was creating, making, and bringing forth (producing) He said in **Genesis 1:26, "Let Us make man in Our image, according to Our likeness; let them have dominion over the fish of the sea, over the birds of the air, and over the cattle, over all the earth and over every creeping thing that creeps on the earth."**

After God created, made, and brought forth man (male and female) He joined and blessed them. He said to them in Genesis 1:28, **"Be fruitful and multiply; fill the earth and subdue it; have dominion over the fish of the sea, over the birds of the air, and over every living thing that moves on the earth."**

Without the two (male and female) the dominion is not full, it is incomplete. The dominion occurs between male and female who agree on the word of God. Dominion does not occur between male and male or between female and female. The dominion occurs when the model on earth resembles the model of the original creator who is male and female. Until male and female are joint together by their creator the blessing that is to increase dominion in the earth is not functioning in its full capacity. What happens in the absence of the blessing is curse or disregard. The curse is free to function in the absence of the blessing. The adversary cannot function in the presence of that blessing. The blessing overtakes him (the adversary). The adversary makes sure when God joins male and female together in a holy matrimony he breaks them up if the man (male and female) allows him. Whether the adversary succeeds or not in separating he also changes the image so even if male and female are joint together the blessing is not functioning. The enemy of our souls will put asunder what God has joint if the joint will permit him. He cannot do anything until he is given the access to do so. Therefore, to keep the blessing functioning apostle Peter in Peter 5:8-9 tells us to "be sober and vigilant because our adversary the devil, as a roaring lion, walks about, seeking whom he may devour. We are to resist him by being steadfast in the faith. Yes, the blessing is with the husband and wife who God joins together, but we are to keep the blessing functioning by our living faith.

Living or Bible's Faith

Living faith is persuasion or conviction plus corresponding action (works). **James 2:20** But do you want to know, O foolish man (male man and female man), that **faith without works** is dead? **James 2:14** What *does it* profit, my brethren, if someone says he has **faith** but does not have **works**? Can **faith** save him? **James 2:18** But someone will say, "You have **faith**, and I have **works**." Show me your **faith without** your **works**, and I will show you my **faith** by my **works**. **James 2:26** For as the body **without** the spirit is dead, so **faith without works** is dead also. **Romans 10:17** - Faith comes by hearing, and hearing by the word of God. **When we speak we hear** ourselves without misunderstanding, error or missing the words we are speaking. When we hear ourselves speaking God's word we gain knowledge of His WILL and MIND by hearing. Our minds get renewed to His WILL and MIND consequently a transformation takes place.

The blessing does not function without a fight, but the good news is that we fight a fixed fight, God has already determined that you are the conqueror if you speak back to Him what He has said about your covenant blessing. Job 4:10 tells us that **the roaring of the lion, and the voice of the fierce lion, and the teeth of the young lions, are broken.** Then in Revelation 12:11 John the revelator tells us that **we overcame him (the devil) by the blood of the Lamb, and by the word of our testimony.** Therefore, we maintain the blessing working by directing our vows and declaration to God so that the blessing may keep functioning in our lives at a very high level every time. We must declare to the devil that his voice that roars like the voice of the fierce lion, and his teeth that may appear like the teeth of the young lions, are broken and cannot hurt our blessing. We make this work when our minds are renewed to the word of God to such a degree that the real events that the enemy causes to appear false and the false events that the enemy causes to appear real are brought to captivity of Christ by 2 Corinthians 10:5 **casting down imaginations, and every high thing that exalts itself against the knowledge of God, and bringing into captivity every thought to the obedience of Christ.**

1 Peter 1:13 tells us to **"gird up the loins of your mind, be sober, and hope to the end for the grace that is to be brought unto you at the revelation of Jesus Christ."**

THE GODHEAD AND MANKIND RELATIONSHIP COMPARISON

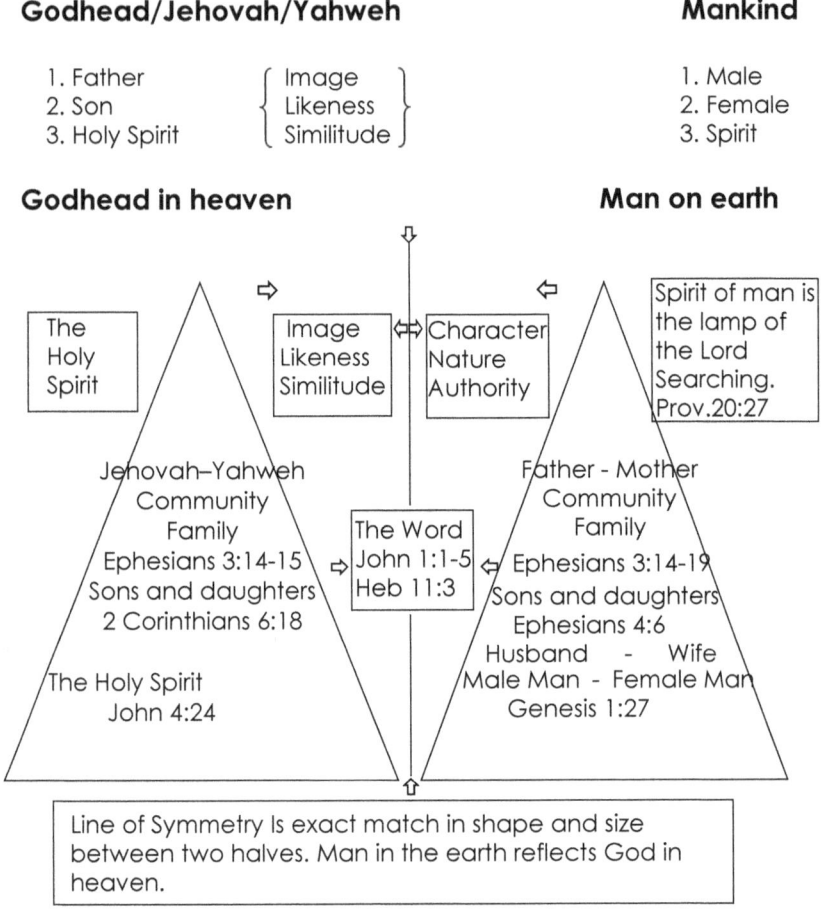

The bible calls Man, male man and woman female man and together they are the man who is the reflection of the Godhead.

Genesis 1:27-28 - **²⁷So God created man in His own image; in the image of God He created him; male and female He created them. ²⁸Then God blessed them, and God said to them, "Be fruitful and multiply; fill the earth and subdue it; have dominion over the fish of the sea, over the birds of the air, and over every living thing that moves on the earth."**

GOD'S ORDER AND PURPOSE OF MARRIAGE

God, the Creator of humanity and of marriage itself, has laid out His plan for marriage as a lifelong union. God knows this design is the best. When we stray from His plan, the results are consequential on many levels.

Unfortunately, the divorce rate in the church is comparable to that of the culture at large. Many Christians see nothing wrong with divorce, at least in their own specific situation, however the Bible clearly addresses marriage and divorce.

Marriage is the first institution God created. God made the first man, Adam, but declared that it was not good for Adam to be alone. He then brought to Adam all the animals, which Adam named, **but "no companion suitable for him" was found.** God was revealing to Adam his completeness was within himself. God then created a wife, Eve, for Adam from within him. He blessed them and their union and gave them the earth to rule over. The creation of marriage occurred prior to sin's entrance into the world. It was a part of God's perfect plan for mankind.

Through the prophets, God emphasized three principles:

1. Marriage is sacred
2. God hates divorce for marriages He has joint Himself
3. Marriage is designed to produce godly seed (children of godly character) that will continue godliness to eternity.

> **Malachi 2:13-16 - And this is the second thing you do: You cover the altar of the Lord with tears, with weeping and crying; So, He does not regard the offering anymore, nor receive it with goodwill from your hands. 14 Yet you say, "For what reason?" Because the Lord has been witness Between you and the wife of your youth, with whom you have dealt treacherously; Yet she is your companion and your wife by covenant. 15 But did He not make them one, Having a remnant of the Spirit?**

> And why one? He seeks godly offspring. Therefore, take heed to your spirit, and let none deal treacherously with the wife of his youth. 16 "For the Lord God of Israel says That He hates divorce, it covers one's garment with violence," Says the Lord of hosts. "Therefore, take heed to your spirit, that you do not deal treacherously."

Jesus underscored the importance and sacredness of lifelong marriage in His own teachings. Have a look at *Matthew 19:6* – **"So then, they are no longer two but one flesh. Therefore, what God has joined together, let not man separate"**

The apostle Paul in Ephesians 5:21-33 further taught that the marital relationship is to be an ongoing demonstration of the sacrificial love that Christ showed His church.

Sadly, God did not join many marriages together. Most couples chose each other blindly in ignorance, leaning on their own understanding, feelings, walking by sight and never by faith. Some eloped because of lust of the flesh. Others m0ved in together by naivety. Others had their marriages arranged through traditions of men. Others had children in sin and decided to join themselves together. Others were forced by circumstances to get children, so they could force their way into marriage. Others refused godly counsel and joint themselves together. All these did not permit God to lead them to His plan for marriage. They joint themselves to marriage and missed it. Consequently, they entered a life full of frustration and disappointment setting the stage for great marital unrest. They kicked God out of their marriage. Whatever happens between them in their marriage God is not involved. **Matthew 19:6 – "..Therefore what God has joined together, let not man separate"** is not applicable to them. They did not trust in the LORD with all their hearts for their God assigned mates but leaned on their own understanding and made decisions outside God's plan. They are either unregenerate, ignored, rebelled or were ignorant of acknowledging God in all their ways for His direction into His plan for this matter of paramount importance.

They did not walk by faith, but by their senses. That which is not of faith is sin and all these joining were in sin and separated themselves from God. However, the good news is that God's mercy that endures to all generations and His sufficient grace is available to get them help for the blessing to function in their union.

Chapter 5

Gifts Joint to Purpose

Medical science discovered what God had already made that the male man has both X (female) and Y (male) chromosomes while the female man has X (female)and X (female) chromosomes only. The Dictionary states that *"Chromosomes are The small bodies in the nucleus of a cell that carry the chemical "instructions" for reproduction of the cell. They consist of strands of DNA wrapped in a double helix around a core of proteins. DNA is the acronym for Deoxyribonucleic acid which is basically a nucleic acid that contains the genetic instructions used in the development and functioning of all known living organisms. Each species of plant or animal has a characteristic number of chromosomes. For human beings, for example, it is forty-six. In humans, gender is determined by two chromosomes: an X-chromosome, which is female, and a Y chromosome, which is male"*

That means the male man's chromosomes determine the gender of the off-spring because he carries both X and Y chromosomes. Female man carries X and X chromosomes only.

GOD'S ORDER AND PURPOSE OF MARRIAGE

CHROMOSOMES

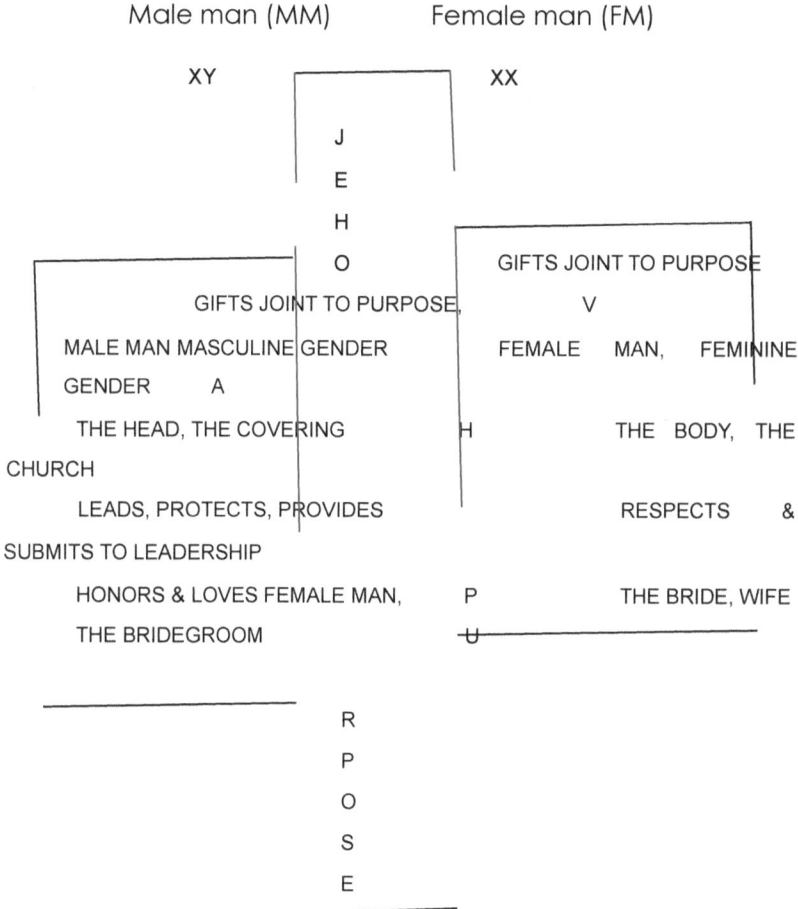

By the above diagram and the word of God we bring clarity to the fact that man is like God in character, nature and authority. God did all His works by speaking and doing what He had spoken. He did not do anything until He first spoke it. Similarly, man is to speak on earth the Word God has spoken in heaven to do it. **Hebrews 11:3 Through faith we understand that the worlds were framed by the word of God, so that things which are seen were not made of things which do appear.**

Therefore, man is to act like God, do what he sees God do and do on earth what he sees the Godhead do in heaven. Both God and man are to function similarly by using the *Word of God*.

John 1:1-5 - ¹**In the beginning was the Word, and the Word was with God, and the Word was God. ²He was with God in the beginning. ³Through him all things were made; without him nothing was made that has been made. ⁴In him was life, and that life was the light of men. ⁵The light shines in the darkness, but the darkness has not understood it.**

God is referred to as FATHER in **Luke 10:21 KJV .... that hour Jesus rejoiced in spirit, and said, I thank thee, O Father, Lord of heaven and earth, that thou hast hid these things from the wise and prudent, and hast revealed them unto babes: even so, Father; for so it seemed good in thy sight.**

Male Man is a Father

God speaking to Abraham said in **Genesis 17:4 KJV ⁴As for me, behold, my covenant is with thee, and you shall be a father of many nations.**

We see Paul making reference to the promises of God to Abraham in Genesis 13:16, Genesis 15:5, Genesis 17:19, ,Genesis 24:7, and Genesis 28:14. said in Romans 4:18 ¹⁸Who against hope believed in hope, that he might become the father of many nations, according to that which was spoken , So shall thy seed be.

Jesus The Christ is Referred as SON

> Matthew 17:5 "While he was still speaking, a bright cloud enveloped them, and a voice from the cloud said, 'This is my Son, whom I love; with him I am well pleased. Listen to him!'"

When both male man and female man are born again God calls them sons.

> **Galatians 4:6 NIV 6 Because you are sons, God sent the Spirit of his Son into our hearts, the Spirit who calls out, "Abba", Father."**
>
> **Romans 8:14 KJV 14 For as many as are led by the Spirit of God, they are the sons of God.**
>
> **1 John 3:2 Beloved, now are we the sons of God, and it doth not yet appear what we shall be : but we know that, when he shall appear , we shall be like him; for we shall see him as he is.**

1. Psalm 54:4 Behold, <u>God</u> is mine helper : the Lord is with them that uphold my soul.

The Holy Spirit Is Our Helper

2. Hebrews 13:6 So that we may boldly say , The Lord is my helper, and I will not fear what man shall do unto me.
3. John 14:16 - And I will pray the Father, and He will give you another Helper, that He may abide with you forever
4. John 14:26 - But the Helper, the Holy Spirit, whom the Father will send in My name, He will teach you all things, and bring to your remembrance all things that I said to you.
5. John 15:26 - But when the Helper comes, whom I shall send to you from the Father, the Spirit of truth who proceeds from the Father, He will testify of Me
6. John 16:7 - Nevertheless I tell you the truth. It is to your advantage that I go away; for if I do not go away, the Helper will not come to you; but if I depart, I will send Him to you.

Female Man Is A Help Meet (helper)

Genesis 2:18 **¹⁸And the Lord God said, "It is not good that man should be alone; I will make him a Help Meet comparable to him."**

Comparable to him denotes complimentary – different, but together form a useful or attractive combination of skills and qualities, Equal, Equivalent, Similar - able to compare, Having Physical features in common to permit comparison.

Male man is not superior to female man and female man is not inferior to male man. They simply have distinct roles and functions.

The purpose for marriage is for fulfillment of God's **PURPOSE** on earth by man being on earth, what God is in heaven. God gave man **GIFTS** to equip him for the Purpose, assignment, and ministry He had commissioned him to do.

The Gifts are connected to Jehovah and wrapped around Him to fulfill His purpose.

He gave both male man and female man each unique and comparable gifts that would work altogether to accomplish His will.

The Godhead and mankind are similar in their functionality. God spoke His Word to create and to bring forth. Jesus The Christ and our Lord spoke the Word to create and to bring forth.

John 5:36 - for the works which the Father hath given me to finish, the same works that I do, bear witness of me, that the Father hath sent Me.

John 5:20 For the Father loves the Son and shows Him all things that Himself does: and He will show him greater works than these.

Similarly, man is to speak the Word of God to create and to bring forth.

Luke 7:5-8 ...... ⁷ But say the word, and my servant will be healed. ⁸ For I also am a man placed under authority, having soldiers under me. And I say to one, 'Go,' and he goes; and to another, 'Come,' and he comes; and to my servant, 'Do this,' and he does it."

Daniel 11:32 ...; but the people that do know their God shall be strong, and do exploits.

Revelation 12:11 And they overcame him by the blood of the Lamb and by the word of their testimony of Jesus The Christ...

Mark 16:17-18 - ¹⁷ And these signs shall follow them that believe; In my name shall they cast out devils; they shall speak with new tongues; ¹⁸ They shall take up serpents; and if they drink any deadly thing, it shall not hurt them; they shall lay hands on the sick, and they shall recover.

The common denominator here is **speaking the Word of God purposely to create and to bring forth** because as He is in heaven so are we in the earth. We are to say/speak the Word to infirmities and expect them to change/be healed. We are to speak our husbands and wives to Destiny, the Purpose, the Assignment and the Ministry God brought them forth to manifest.

1 John 4:17 ...; because as He is, so are we in this world .

God commands order and control/dominion where He is and we are to have order and control/dominion where we are. "Like the father like the son"

The Father in heaven gets things done by speaking, so ought the earthly father (Male man) by speaking what God Spoke to the circumstance and diseases to bring order in the earth.

Then Jesus as a Son gets things done by speaking what The Father Spoke, so ought the adopted sons (Male and Female man) get things done by speaking what The Father Spoke to the circumstance.

The Holy Spirit gets things done by speaking what God Spoke, so ought the spirit man (Male and Female man) get things done by speaking what The Father Spoke to the circumstance.

Just like all of us learn our familial languages, when we get born again we must learn godly familial language so we can speak on earth the same thing God has spoken in heaven and get the same results The Father has gotten. Speech is inclusive of voice sounds and deeds.

Before we can go farther let us first define what language is so we can effectively communicate with God:

Language is a human system of communication that uses arbitrary signals, such as voice sounds, gestures, or written symbols.

However, language is complicated, intriguing, and mysterious to be adequately explained by a brief definition. Language is the armory or arsenal of the human mind, and at once contains the trophies of its past and the weapons of its future conquests. **Language is an art.** Every language must be learnt except speaking in tongues which is given by the Holy Spirit. It differs, however, widely from all ordinary arts, for man has an instinctive tendency to speak. Language is slowly and unconsciously developed by many steps.

The prayers that get you results or God answers are prayers that are inclusive of the language of God (Word of God). We have included herein examples of what we call Word prayers. My Wife Jedidah and I pray for each other in our private personal time of prayer so we can stay focused in our purpose in God.

Jesus our Lord said in **John 15:7 - If you abide in me, and my words abide in you, you shall ask what you will, and it shall be done unto you.**

We abide in God and His Word abides in us by prayerfully speaking God's Word to everything and situation that speaks to us contrary to His Word. In our regular communication with our fellow men and women we are to make sure that we are speaking the language of God to get done what we ask of the Father in heaven.

Amos 3:3 Can two walk together, except they be agreed?

Amos 3:2-4 - You only have I known of all the families of the earth: therefore, I will punish you for all your iniquities Can two walk together, except they be agreed? Will a lion roar in the forest, when he hath no prey? will a young lion cry out of his den, if he has taken nothing?)

Psalm 37:14 The wicked have drawn out the sword, and have bent their bow, to cast down the poor and needy, and to slay such as be of upright conversation.

Psalm 37:13-15 [13] The LORD shall laugh at him: for he sees that his day is coming. [14] The wicked have drawn out the sword, and have bent their bow, to cast down the poor and needy, and to slay such as be of upright conversation. [15] Their sword shall enter into their own heart, and their bows shall be broken.

Psalm 50:23 Whoso offers praise glorifies me: and to him that orders his conversation aright will I shew the salvation of God. (In context [22] Now consider this, ye that forget God, lest I tear you in pieces, and there be none to deliver. [23] Whoso offers praise glorifies me: and to him that orders his conversation aright will I shew the salvation of God.

2 Corinthians 1:12 For our rejoicing is this, the testimony of our conscience, that in simplicity and godly sincerity, not with fleshly wisdom, but by the grace of God, we have had our conversation in the world, and more abundantly to you-ward.

2 Corinthians 1:11-13 [11] Ye also helping together by prayer for us, that for the gift bestowed upon us by the means of many persons thanks may be given by many on our behalf. [12] For our rejoicing is this, the testimony of our conscience, that in simplicity and godly sincerity, not with fleshly wisdom, but by the grace of God, we have had our conversation in the world, and more abundantly to you-ward. [13] For we write none other things unto you, than what ye read or acknowledge; and I trust ye shall acknowledge even to the end

Galatians 1:13 For ye have heard of my conversation in time past in the Jews' religion, how that beyond measure I persecuted the church of God, and wasted it:

Ephesians 2:3 Among whom also we all had our conversation in times past in the lusts of our flesh, fulfilling the desires of the flesh and of the mind; and were by nature the children of wrath, even as others.

Ephesians 4:22 That ye put off concerning the former conversation the old man, which is corrupt according to the deceitful lusts

Philippians 1:27 Only let your conversation be as it becometh the gospel of Christ: that whether I come and see you, or else be absent, I may hear of your affairs, that ye stand fast in one spirit, with one mind striving together for the faith of the gospel

Philippians 3:20 For our conversation is in heaven; from whence also we look for the Savior, the Lord Jesus Christ.

GOD'S ORDER AND PURPOSE OF MARRIAGE

1 Timothy 4:12 Let no man despise thy youth; but be thou an example of the believers, in word, in conversation, in charity, in spirit, in faith, in purity.

Hebrews 13:5 ⁴Marriage is honorable in all, and the bed undefiled: but whoremongers and adulterers God will judge. ⁵Let your conversation be without covetousness; and be content with such things as ye have: for he hath said, I will never leave thee, nor forsake thee. ⁶So that we may boldly say, The Lord is my helper, and I will not fear what man shall do unto me.

Hebrews 13:5-7 ⁵Let your conversation be without covetousness; and be content with such things as ye have: for he hath said, I will never leave thee, nor forsake thee. ⁶So that we may boldly say, The Lord is my helper, and I will not fear what man shall do unto me. ⁷Remember them which have the rule over you, who have spoken unto you the word of God: whose faith follow, considering the end of their conversation.

James 3:13 Who is a wise man and endued with knowledge among you? let him shew out of a friendly conversation his works with meekness of wisdom.

1 Peter 1:15 But as he which hath called you is holy, so be ye holy in all manner of conversation;

1 Peter 1:18 Forasmuch as ye know that ye were not redeemed with corruptible things, as silver and gold, from your vain conversation received by tradition from your fathers;

1 Peter 2:12 Having your conversation honest among the Gentiles: that, whereas they speak against you as evildoers, they may by your good works, which they shall behold, glorify God in the day of visitation.

1 Peter 3:1 Likewise, ye wives, be in subjection to your own husbands; that, if any obey not the word, they also may without the word be won by the conversation of the wives

1 Peter 3:2 While they behold your chaste conversation coupled with fear.

1 Peter 3:16 Having a good conscience; that, whereas they speak evil of you, as of evildoers, they may be ashamed that falsely accuse your good conversation in Christ.

2 Peter 2:7 And delivered just Lot, vexed with the filthy conversation of the wicked.

2 Peter 3:11 Seeing then that all these things shall be dissolved, what manner of persons ought ye to be in all holy conversation and godliness.

Chapter 6

Household Prayers

The head of the household whether husband, wife or single parent, it is your privilege and duty to pray for the household in your charge and those under your care and authority. The reason a wife can be head of household is because when husbands relinquish their responsibilities and obligations leaving the family uncovered and exposed to the adversary's attack, the wife will not sit back and watch destruction of her family. It is proper, it is fitting, and it is right for her to take over and become the covering for her family.

In 1 Cor. 11:3-15, "a woman ought to have a symbol of authority on her head because of the angels. "Covering" is a kind of metaphor for husbands being the head and the wife coming under his wings. An ancient Hebrew wedding custom included a robe or shawl that the groom placed around the shoulders of his bride signifying she has come under his covenant covering of protection, and spiritual, physical, emotional, and material care."

Covering is like the blood that covers our sins. A husband is the head and the responsibility fall on him. As Jesus took the responsibility for our sins and to protect us from the wrath that sin will inflect on us. So, a husband is to cover his wife and family by this same love and sacrifice that it takes to care for his family. A wife is a help-meet which means partner. She should be treated as an equal and not less. The husband should respect his wife's opinion and she should respect his godly spiritual leadership. If there is no godly leadership, there is no submission. We submit to God through those who lead in godliness.

James 4:7 - Therefore submit to God. Resist the devil and he will flee from you.

There are things that God has given each of us that the others cannot see. We need to have wisdom to know the difference and walk in it. The word of God in Genesis 3:1-13, 16, and 1 Timothy 2:14 states, in the beginning, God placed the wife under the protective covering of her husband and took responsibility away from her placing it on the husband, because it was the female man who had been deceived.

According to *Titus 2:4-5,* older women are instructed to behave properly and to instruct younger women to love their husbands and children, to be discreet, chaste, homemakers, good, obedient to their own husbands, that the word of God may not be blasphemed.

Conforming to the word of God in Ephesians 5:22, Colossians 3:18, and 1 Peter 3:1, the only command God gave to the wife is to submit to godly leadership (as unto the Lord) of her husband. God does not require the wife to submit to husband's ungodly leadership. God will hold the husband responsible for failure of being a covering to her. In Ephesians 5:25-33, Colossians 3:18-19, 1 Peter 3:7 God commands the husband to be responsible for his wife in a loving and cherishing role. If the wife has no father or husband to provide this covering, then she bears her own responsibility before God. God loves the wife, and His best desire is for her to have the protective covering of a loving father or loving husband. Often in today's society, the wife finds herself having to assume the responsibility and position of the head of the household.

Prayer Blessing the Household

As the head of the family it is your privilege and duty to pray for the household in your charge and those under your care and authority.

Head of household could be a male man or female man. So often in our today's society, the woman finds herself having to assume the responsibility and position of the head of the household. This prayer of faith will make tremendous power available to help in every area of need in the household. Prayer of faith is praying the word of God on the matter.

Prayer

Revelation 1:6: Father, as the priest and the head of my household, I declare and decree Joshua 24:15 "As for me and my house we shall serve the Lord"

Ephesians 1:3: Praise be to You, God and Father of our Lord Jesus Christ, for you have blessed us in heavenly realms with every spiritual blessing in Christ. John 4:23 We reverence You and Worship You in Spirit and in truth.

Matthew 18:20: Lord we acknowledge and welcome the presence of Your Holy Spirit here in our home. We thank You, Father, that Your Son, Jesus, is here with us because we are gathered together in His name.

2 Peter 1:3: Lord God, Your divine power has given to us everything that *pertain* to life and godliness, through our knowledge of You who called us by your own glory and goodness.

Psalm 112:2: As the spiritual leader of my home, I declare by the authority of your word that my descendants (family) is mighty on earth; This generation of the upright is blessed.

Psalm 35:27: Father, we are shouting for joy and we are glad, because we favor Your righteous cause; And we continually say, " Lord be magnified, for You find pleasure in our prosperity."

Psalm 112:3: Lord, we declare and decree Wealth and riches *is* in our house, And our righteousness endures forever.

Psalm 25:13: Lord, I declare I myself dwell in prosperity, and my descendants are inheriting the earth.

Psalm 118:25: Lord Save now, I pray, O Lord; O Lord, I pray, send now prosperity to us.

Prayer of Blessing at the Table

The head of the household leads in thanking God for meals, blessing the meals and sanctifying the meals that God has provided knowing that according to James 1:17 every good gift and every perfect gift is from above, and comes down from the Father of lights, with whom there is no variation or shadow of turning. He or she is to thank and praise God for His blessing of food and to cleanse and consecrate it before it is received. Also, Household head gets the opportunity to sanctify the family members who partake of the food.

Prayer

Matthew 6:11 - Father, thank You for giving us this day our daily bread both spiritual and physical.

1 Timothy 4:4 - We break and receive this bread with thanksgiving and praise because every creature of God *is* good, and nothing is to be refused if it is received with thanksgiving.

Exodus 23:25 - You Lord, God bless our bread and our water, and You take sickness away from our midst.

Mark 16:18 - In the name of Jesus, we call this food sanctified, wholesome, and pure nourishment to our bodies. We declare nothing deadly can hurt us, Romans 8:2 - for the law of the Spirit of life in Christ Jesus has made us free from the law of sin and death.

In the name of Jesus, Amen.

Wife's Prayer for Self and Husband

Hebrews 10:19-23 - Father, this is Your son, (Your name) coming to You by the blood of Your Son, my Lord and Savior Jesus The Christ that gives me access to your presence, Hallelujah…

Hebrews 4:16 – I boldly come to Your throne of grace to obtain mercy and find grace to help in time of need. I receive my today's new mercies and I walk in it. I am finding grace and I am getting help with every need.

I enter my today's promise and receive my today's good news.

Proverbs 3:3-4 – I declare mercy and truth do not forsake me. I bind them around my neck, write them on the tablet of my heart, and I find favor and high esteem in Your sight O God and man.

Psalm 103:2-5 – Father, I bless Your Holy name and do not forget all Your benefits to me. I declare I am loaded with your blessing. You forgive me of all transgressions, heal me of all diseases (Something that is very wrong with people's attitudes, way of life, or with Society: Greed is a disease of modern society), and redeem my life from destructions. You crown me with your loving kindness and tender mercies. You satisfy my mouth with Your good Word and renew my youth like the eagles.

Deuteronomy 34:7 My eyes do not get dim nor my natural **vigor** diminish.

1 Peter 3:1-6 – Father, in the name of Jesus I cultivate inner beauty, the gentle gracious kind that You delight in just like the holy women of old were beautiful before You, and were good, loyal wives to their husbands. I obey my husband Like Sarah obeyed Abraham and called him lord whose daughter I am. I do well and my conversation to my husband is with grace coupled with salt calling him lord. I resist the temptation of becoming anxious and intimidated. Whenever I speak I have something worthwhile to say, and I say it with kindness.

Ephesians 5:22, 33 - Father in the name of Jesus the Christ, I purpose to understand and support my husband in ways that show my support for Christ. As the church is totally responsive to Christ, in the same way I respond to my husband in every respect of our relationship. My husband purposes to understand and love me, his wife, in ways that show Christ's love for him. As Christ totally loves the church, in the same way my husband loves me, his wife in every respect of our relationship. My husband is providing leadership to me the way Christ does to His church, not by domineering, but by cherishing me. He goes all out in his love for me, exactly as Christ did for the Church – a love marked by giving, not getting. My husband and I are the body of Christ, and by loving me, he loves himself.

Romans 12:2 - I am being transformed by the renewing of my entire mind, and I am a good wife to my husband, appropriately responsive to his needs, proving Your good, and acceptable, and perfect will. I thank You for my inner disposition that is reflecting Your glory. Hallelujah......

2 Corinthians 3:18 By Your Grace Father, I yield to the constant ministry of transformation from glory to glory by the Holy Spirit. **Proverbs 12:4** - I am being transformed into a gracious woman who retains honor and a virtuous woman who is a crown to my husband. **Proverbs 14:1** I'm purposely walking wisely building my house. **Proverbs 19:14** - I am a prudent (careful and sensitive in making judgements/determinations/decisions); (care, caution, and good judgment, as well as wisdom in looking ahead) wife from You, Lord to my husband. **Ephesians 1:7-8** - In Christ I have redemption through His blood, the forgiveness of sins, according to the riches of His grace which He made to abound toward me with all wisdom and prudence (avoiding unnecessary risks).

Matthew 16:19 - I have the keys of the kingdom of heaven: and all that I'm binding on earth is being bound in heaven: and whatsoever I'm losing on earth You, Father are losing it in heaven.

GOD'S ORDER AND PURPOSE OF MARRIAGE

1 Corinthians 7:2-5 - Father, I thank You for teaching me to function so that I preserve my own personality while responding to desires of my husband. My husband and I are one flesh and I understand this unity of persons that preserves individuality is a mystery, but that is how it is when we are united to Christ. So I keep on loving my husband and the miracle keeps on happening. My husband gives me what is due me and I seek to be fair to my husband. I share my rights with my husband.

Proverbs 31:10 - Father, I am a capable, intelligent, and virtuous woman. My worth is far more precious than jewels, and my value is far above rubies or pearls.

Proverb 31:25-27 – Strength and dignity are my clothing, and my position is secure and strong in my household. My family is in readiness for the future. The bread of idleness (gossip, discontent, and self-pity) I will not eat. I choose to conduct the affairs of my household wisely, realizing that wisdom from above is pure, peaceable, gentle, willing to yield, full of mercy and good fruits, without partiality and without hypocrisy. I open my mouth with skillful and godly wisdom, and on my tongue is the law of kindness (giving counsel and instruction).

Proverbs 31:28-29 – Our children rise up and call me, (your name) blessed (empowered to prosper, happy and to be envied). My husband boast of and praises me (saying), "Many daughters have done virtuously, nobly, and well (with the strength of character that is steadfast in goodness), but you excel them all." Yes, I agree with Your word and my husband that I excel them all.

Proverbs 31:30-31 – Father, I reverently and worshipfully fear You and I am praised. I have the fruit of the work of my hands. My own works praise me in the gate of the city.

Psalm 112:1-4 - Father, I delight greatly in Your commandments, and my descendants are mighty on earth. I am upright and my generation is empowered to prosper, happy, and envied. I declare wealth and riches are in our house, and our righteousness endures forever. I am upright and I bring light in the darkness: I am gracious, and full of compassion, and righteous.

Acts 27:25 - Father, I receive my declarations fulfilled just as it was told me, and I walk in them.

Luke 1:38 - Father, behold Your daughter; it is unto me according to Your word.

Mark 11:23b - I receive my proclamation/*declaration relative to how my husband and I are to relate to each other. I thank you for Luke 1:45; Philippians 1:6; Ezekiel 12:25 - performance of your word in my marriage.*

In Jesus' name, Amen

Husband's Prayer for Wife and Himself

It is positive reinforcement, validation, and affirmation for children to hear their father pray, blessing his wife and their mother. This is a way for honoring her and reaffirming her position in the home. Words are powerful, and the blessing for the wife before the children will promote appropriate self-esteem necessary for success in life.

Sometimes a wife will feel that she has failed because she is not fulfilling all the roles expressed in proverbs 31. I believe that God had this chapter written to encourage a woman to be all that He created her to be. Out of her being, knowing herself, both her strengths and her weaknesses, developing her talents, seeing herself as God sees her, and looking to Christ for her completeness, comes in the doing.

The woman described in in proverbs 31 has outstanding abilities. Her family's social position is high. In fact, she may not be one woman at all. She may be a composite portrait of ideal womanhood. Do not see her as a model to imitate in every detail. Your days are not long enough to do everything she does! See her instead as an inspiration to be all you can be. Ladies can't just be like her, but they can learn from her industry, integrity, and resourcefulness.

Prayer

Hebrews 10:19-23 - Father, this is your son, (Your name) coming to You by the blood of Your Son Jesus the Christ that gives me access to your presence, Hallelujah…

Hebrews 4:16 – I boldly come to Your throne of grace and I am obtaining mercy and finding grace to help in time of need. I receive my today's new mercies and I am walking in it. Father I thank You that I am finding grace and I am getting help with every need.

Proverbs 3:3-4 – Father, I declare mercy and truth do not forsake me. I bind them around my neck, write them on the tablet of my heart, and I find favor and high esteem in Your sight O God and man.

Psalm 103:2-5 – Father, I bless Your Holy name and do not forget all Your benefits to me. You forgive me of all transgressions, heal me of all diseases, and redeem my life from destructions. You crown me with your loving kindness and tender mercies. You satisfy my mouth with Your good Word and renew my youth like the eagles.

Deuteronomy 34:7 - I declare my vigor does not diminish neither my eye sight go dim.

Genesis 2:18 – Father, in the beginning You made for me, a helpmeet, companion, partner - my wife. Now, Father when Proverbs 18:22 - I found (wife's name) as my wife, help meet, companion, and partner I found **a good thing** and obtained favor from You, Lord.

Ephesians 5:22, 33 - Father in the name of Jesus the Christ, I purpose to understand and love my wife in ways that show Christ's love for me. As Christ totally loves the church, in the same way I love my wife (wife's name) in every respect of our relationship. I am providing leadership to my wife, (wife's name) the way Christ does to His church, not by domineering, but by cherishing her. I go all out in my love for her, exactly as Christ did for the Church – a love marked by giving, not getting. My wife, (wife's name) and I are the body of Christ, and by loving her, I love myself.

1 Corinthians 7:2-5 –Father, I thank You for teaching me to function so that I preserve my own personality while responding to desires of my wife, (wife's name). My wife, (wife's name) and I are one flesh and I understand this unity of persons that preserves individuality is a mystery, but that is how it is when we are united to Christ. So I keep on loving my wife, (wife's name) and the miracle keeps on happening. My wife, (wife's name) gives me what is due me and I seek to be fair to my wife, (wife's name). I share my rights with my wife, (wife's name).

1 Peter 3:7-9 I honor my wife, (wife's name) and delight in her. In the new life of grace, we are equals. I treat my wife, (wife's name) as an equal to me and all our prayers are always answered.

1 Peter 3:1-6 – Father, in the name of Jesus my wife cultivates inner beauty, the gentle gracious kind that You delight in. The holy women of old were beautiful before You Father, and were good, loyal wives to their husbands. Sarah obeyed Abraham calling him lord. My wife (wife's name) is a holy woman and very beautiful before You, Father. My wife (Wife's name) is Sarah's daughter because she does well and calls me her lord. Our conversation to each other is with grace coupled with salt. She resists the temptation of becoming anxious and intimidated. Whenever we speak to each other we have something worthwhile to say, and we say it with kindness.

Proverbs 31:10 - Father, I thank You for my wife, (wife's name). She is a capable, intelligent, and virtuous woman. Her worth is far more precious than jewels, and her value is far above rubies or pearls.

Proverbs 31:25-26 – Father, I declare my wife, (wife's name) is a woman of strong character, great wisdom, many skills, and great compassion. Strength and dignity are her clothing, and her position is strong and secure in our household. She opens her mouth with skillful and godly wisdom, and on her tongue is the law of kindness (giving counsel and instruction).

Proverbs 31:28-29 – Our children rise up and call my wife, (wife's name) blessed (empowered to prosper, happy and to be envied) and I boast of and praise her. Father, it is true that many daughters have done virtuously, nobly, and well (with the strength of character that is steadfast in goodness), but my wife (wife's name) excels them all."

Proverbs 31:30-31 – Father, my wife, (wife's name) reverently and worshipfully fears You and she is praised. She has the fruit of the work of her hands. Her own works praises her in the gate of the city.

Psalm 112:1-4 - Father, my wife (wife's name) delight greatly in Your commandments, and our descendants are mighty on earth. My wife (wife's name) and I are upright and our generation is empowered to prosper. I declare wealth and riches are in our house, and our righteousness endures forever. I declare my wife (wife's name) and I are upright and we bring light in the darkness: we are gracious, full of compassion, and righteous.

Romans 12:2 – I'm being transformed by the renewing of my entire mind, and I am a loving husband to my wife (wife's name), appropriately responsive to her needs proving Your good, and acceptable, and perfect will. I thank You for my inner disposition that is reflecting Your glory.

2 Corinthians 3:18 By Your grace Father, I yield to the constant ministry of transformation from glory to glory by the Holy Spirit.

Matthew 16:19 - I have the keys of the kingdom of heaven: and all that I'm binding on earth is being bound in heaven: and whatsoever I'm loosing on earth You, Father, You are loosing it in heaven.

Acts 27:25 - Father, I receive my declarations fulfilled just as it was told me, and I walk in them. **Luke 1:38** Father, behold Your son; it is unto me according to Your word Jeremiah 1:12 because you hasten/watch over it to perform it.

> I declare that, I conduct myself so as to bring glory to God, honor and respect to my wife, the Brotherhood and the respect & confidence of my family, friends, peers and strangers.
>
> Lord I declare that, I provide vision, direction and leadership for my wife and family. I place their needs above my own. I love my wife as Christ loved the Church. I protect my daughters and mentor my sons. I faithfully serve the Church, my country and my community.
>
> Lord I declare, my life exemplifies loyalty, discipline, fidelity and bravery.
>
> I refuse to compromise my integrity, nor blemish my character through illicit activities or immoral behavior. I do not cower under to the pressures of life, nor will I yield to temptations that would hurt my family or bring dishonor to my name.
>
> For me, failure or excuses are not an option. I carryout and I fulfill my God-given purpose on planet earth.
>
> At all times, and in all circumstances and situations, I demonstrate courage born of the Holy Spirit, guts tempered by chapter and verse, spiritual strength and mental prowess emanating from fervent prayer and faith in the Written Word of God.
>
> I am a strong man, strong in the Lord and in the power of His might, who speaks the truth in love. I am an honorable

man, a leader, a gentleman, bold and yet humble, patient and intelligent, a man of chivalry, a man who walks tenderly before the Lord God. I am a man who is Mastering Manhood.

By these convictions I live and by these convictions I stand.

In Jesus name, Amen.

Chapter 7

Man's (male and female) self-rule

Genesis 1:28 ²⁸ Then God blessed them, and God said to them, "Be fruitful and multiply; fill the earth and subdue it; have dominion over the fish of the sea, over the birds of the air, and over every living thing that moves on the earth.

Genesis 2:8-9 – God Himself planted a garden and put in the man He had formed.

Genesis 2:15 God assigned the man the ministry of tending and keeping it.

Genesis 2:17 The autonomy (the ability to act and make decisions without being controlled by anyone else) is recognized in God's warning: "You shall surely die"

Man's self-rule is all inclusive of Spiritual death, Moral death, Relational death, Social death, and ultimately physical death.

The male man gets help to fulfill his assignment, ministry, purpose from many sources:

1. The Lord – Hebrews 13:6; Psalm 54:4,
2. The Holy Spirit – John 14:16,
3. The Angels – Hebrews 1:13-14, Psalm 103:19-21

4. The female man (help meet) - Genesis 2:18
5. Obtaining Gods Mercy - Hebrews 4:16a
6. Finding Gods Great Grace - Hebrews 4:16b

The male man needs to speak the word of God to whatever he wants to happen, and the angels will do it in his favor.

Hebrews 1:13-14 "[13] But to which of the angels has He ever said: "Sit at My right hand, Till I make Your enemies Your footstool"? [14] Are they not all ministering spirits sent forth to minister for those who will inherit salvation?"

Psalm 103:19-21 – "[19] The LORD hath prepared his throne in the heavens; and his kingdom rules over all. [20] Bless the LORD, ye his angels, that excel in strength, that do his commandments, hearkening unto the voice of his word." and the female man (help meet) - *Genesis 2:18* 18

Genesis 2:18 **18 - And the Lord God said, "It is not good that man should be alone; I will make him a help MEET comparable to him."**

The Wife is not a servant, but a help meets. She provides the help needed to get needs met.

Genesis 2:18 indicates that Adam's (male man's) strength for all he was called to be and do was inadequate in itself.

The help the female man meets is for: Ministry – Daily work, Raising godly seed – Procreation (Reproduction), and Purpose – Mutual support through companionship.

Comparable to him

The phrase "Comparable to him" denotes Complimentary – different, but together form a useful or attractive combination of skills and qualities ie Equal, Equivalent, Similar - able to compare, Having Physical features in common to permit comparison. The Male man is not superior to the female man and the female man is not inferior to the male man. They simply have dissimilar roles, responsibilities, and functions.

Gen. 2:19-20 –** [19] **Out of the ground the Lord God formed every beast of the field and every bird of the air and brought them to Adam to see what he would call them. And whatever Adam called each living creature, that was its name.** [20] **So Adam gave names to all cattle, to the birds of the air, and to every beast of the field. But for Adam there was not found a helper comparable to him.

Genesis 2:19 – "That Was Its Name"

Jehovah brought every beast of the field and every bird of the air which He had already named to Adam to see what he would call them. And whatever Adam called each living creature that was its name Jehovah had given it.

"**That Was Its Name**" - restates what God had already instructed man in **Genesis 1:28** to have dominion over the earth and its creatures.

Genesis 1:28 **"… have dominion over the fish of the sea, over the birds of the air, and over every living thing that moves on the earth."**

God was checking to confirm the man he had made had His deoxyribonucleic acid (**DNA**). In other words, God was checking to see whether the man He had made resembled Him in character, nature and authority. Mankind is supposed to take dominion or rule, think, act, speak like his Creator relative to marriage relationship just like in everything else. This is only possible when he is in right standing or relationship with his Maker. Romans 12:2 tells us that we get into right relationship with God by being forgiven of sin and always being transformed by the **renew**ing of our **mind** to continue being in that good and acceptable and perfect will of God

To continue embracing God's purpose for marriage and honoring marital fidelity, it is crucial that in marriage deeds we hear Christ and be taught by Him the truth in Jesus about marriage relationship. The TRUTH in Jesus about marriage is being renewed in the spirit of our mind and putting on the new man which was created according to God, in true righteousness and holiness. If in deeds we have done according to the truth in Jesus that we heard Christ say and teach relative to marriage affairs we shall be graced to *put off, concerning your former conduct, the old man which grows corrupt according to the deceitful lusts.* Jesus is the bridegroom to the church

Ephesians 4:20-24 [20] But you have not so learned Christ, [21] if indeed you have heard Him and have been taught by Him, as the truth is in Jesus: [22] that you put off, concerning your former conduct, the old man which grows corrupt according to the deceitful lusts, [23] and be renewed in the spirit of your mind, [24] and that you put on the new man which was created according to God, in true righteousness and holiness.

The one in authority is entitled to name the members of community for which he is responsible. A name is not merely a convenient conglomeration of letters. Rather the name reveals its essential characteristic. It is a defining piece of one's identity for a lifetime. Adam looked into the essence of every creature and named it accordingly the names God had named them. On the same token Adam named the female man "Woman"

Genesis 2:23 And Adam said: "This is now bone of my bones And flesh of my flesh; She shall be called Woman, Because she was taken out of Man."

It is important to choose a name that will have a positive effect, since every time it is used the person is reminded of its meaning.

Genesis 17:15-16 ¹⁵ Then God said to Abraham, "As for Sarai your wife, you shall not call her name Sarai, but Sarah *shall be* her name. ¹⁶ And I will bless her and give you a son by her; then I will bless her, and she shall be *a mother of* nations; kings of peoples shall be from her."

No doubt the import of naming members of family cannot be over emphasized because a person's name is a title which says something about him or her and is essential for communicating with them.

Genesis 5:29 And he called his name Noah, saying, "This one will comfort us concerning our work and the toil of our hands, because of the ground which the Lord has cursed."

It is an adornment and symbol for the person, by which he is called in this world.

Genesis 17:5 No longer shall your name be called Abram, but your name shall be Abraham; for I have made you a father of many nations.

It is indicative of the individual's future and speaks of what they will turn out to become. It gives an impression of him to other people.

Genesis 3:20 And Adam called his wife's name Eve, because she was the mother of all living.

"One of his Ribs"

Genesis 2:21-22 ²¹ And the LORD God caused a deep sleep to fall on Adam, and he slept; and He took one of his ribs, and closed up the flesh in its place. ²²Then the rib which the LORD God had taken from man He made into a woman, and He brought her to the man."

The **Rib** was chosen as a representative of an **Intimate** part of Adam's makeup. A wife is an intimate part of the husband and **should be treated as such.**

Genesis 2:24 ²⁴ Therefore a man shall Leave his father and mother and be Joined to his wife, and they shall become One Flesh.

"**Leave**" – means a change is priority on the part of the husband.

Be Joined Together means it has the idea of Passion. In this context, it is a strong feeling of loving a wife very much. It means it has the idea of Permanence. The state of lasting for a long time. The state of lasting for all time in the futures.

That means marriage that God has put together is a lasting relationship. There is nothing like separation or divorce. It is the Shalom of God, nothing missing, lacking or broken.

Mark 10:9 Therefore what God has joined together, let not man separate."

Chapter 8

But One Flesh

The statement **But One Flesh** carries a number of implications. Your body and your spirit belong to God. The scripture tells us what **But One Flesh** implies.

1 Corinthians 6:16-20 [16] ..."Or do you not know that he who is joined to a harlot is one body with her? For "the two," He says, "shall become one flesh."[a] [17] But he who is joined to the Lord is one spirit with Him. [18] Flee sexual immorality. Every sin that a man does is outside the body, but he who commits sexual immorality sins against his own body. [19] Or do you not know that your body is the temple of the Holy Spirit who is in you, whom you have from God, and you are not your own? [20] For you were bought at a price; therefore glorify God in your body[b] and in your spirit, which are God's.

Mark 10:8-9 .... [8] and the two shall become one flesh'; [a] so then they are no longer two, but one flesh. [9] Therefore what God has joined together, let not man separate."

Matthew 19:5-6 ... [5] and said, 'For this reason a man shall leave his father and mother and be joined to his wife, and the two shall become one flesh'? [6] So then, they are no longer two but one flesh. Therefore, what God has joined together, let not man separate."

What that means is husband and wife are one in everything; Purpose, Ministry, Assignment, Sexual union, Child conception, Spiritual and emotional intimacy, showing each other the same respect shown to close kin, such as one's parents and siblings. Christians mates are also to each other brother and sister.

Genesis 2:23 - ²³ And Adam said: "This is now bone of my bones And flesh of my flesh; She shall be called Woman, Because she was taken out of Man."

The male man admires beauty. The male man is visual. The male man is attracted by beauty. What the male man sees stays in him (in his mind) until he replaces it with something else. The male man is pleased by kindness. The male man looks for support, happiness, and peace from his wife. The male man wants to entrust his wealth to his wife.

The term "one flesh" comes from the Genesis account of the creation of Eve.

Genesis 2:21-24 ²¹ "And the LORD God caused a deep sleep to fall on Adam, and he slept; and He took one of his ribs, and closed up the flesh in its place. ²² Then the rib which the LORD God had taken from man He made into a woman, and He brought her to the man. ²³ And Adam said: "This is now bone of my bones And flesh of my flesh; She shall be called Woman, Because she was taken out of Man." ²⁴ Therefore a man shall leave his father and mother and be joined to his wife, and they shall become one flesh"

The above scripture describes the process by which God created Eve from a rib taken from Adam's side as he slept. Adam recognized that Eve was part of him—they were in fact "one flesh." The term "one flesh" would mean that just as our bodies are one whole entity and cannot be divided into pieces and still be a whole, so God intended it to be with the marriage relationship. There are no longer two entities (two individuals), but now there is one entity (a married couple).

There are a number of aspects to this new union. Concerning emotional attachments, the new unit takes precedence over all previous and future relationships.

(Genesis 2:24 *"Therefore a man shall leave his father and mother and be joined to his wife, and they shall become one flesh"*.

Some marriage partners continue to place greater weight upon ties with parents than with the new partner. This is a recipe for disaster in the marriage and is a perversion of God's original intention of "leaving and cleaving." A similar problem can develop when a spouse begins to draw closer to a child to meet emotional needs rather than to his or her partner.

In an ideal marriage situation where God was allowed to join them, the couple is to become one emotionally, spiritually, intellectually, financially, and in every other way. Even as one part of the body cares for the other body parts (the stomach digests food for the body, the brain directs the body for the good of the whole, the hands work for the sake of the body, etc.), so each partner in the marriage is to care for the other. Each partner is no longer to see money earned as "my" money; but rather as "our" money.

(Ephesians 5:22-33 ... For no one ever hated his own flesh, but nourishes and cherishes it, just as the Lord does the church. [30] For we are members of His body,[a] of His flesh and of His bones, and Proverbs 31:10-31 Who[a] can find a virtuous[b] wife? For her worth is far above rubies.[11] The heart of her husband safely trusts her; So he will have no lack of gain.[12] She does him good and not evil All the days of her life.[20] She extends her hand to the poor, Yes, she reaches out her hands to the needy. [26] She opens her mouth with wisdom, and on her tongue is the law of kindness and let her own works praise her in the gates" gives the application of this "oneness" to the role of the husband and to the wife, respectively.

They become one flesh Physically, and the result of that one flesh is found in the children that their union produces; these children now possess a special genetic makeup, specific to the union of husband and wife.

Even so in the sexual aspect of their relationship, a husband and wife are not to consider their bodies as their own but as belonging to their partner. This is not to be misconstrued to mean wives are sex objects and must avail themselves to their husbands every time without consideration as if they don't have feelings and right to their bodies specially in an abusive situation. Like everything else sexual intercourse has its right moment all things considered.

The book of **Ecclesiastes 3:1 in the bible says -"To everything there is a season, A time for every purpose under heaven."** There are things and times that precede emotional readiness for sexual activity particularly to wives. The bible speaks of those times in Ecclesiastes **3:3-8. A time to heal her wounded heart and broken Spirit.**

"Proverbs 17:22 - A merry heart does good, like medicine, But a broken spirit dries the bones." When her spirit is broken she is dry and no penetration can occur without hurting her.

A time to build up her self-esteem to better your relationship.

A wife is the best thing that could ever happen to anyone and if a man mistreats her, he will miss out on a good thing. In a time when women are faced with many outside demands of career, family, and community their understanding spiritual husbands will give them the tools and inspiration needed to remain grounded. If a husband is detached and egocentric, you believing wife look to the Father and start building the foundation of a healthy self-esteem on the word of God to cultivate essential key practices or virtues; living consciously, self-acceptance, self-responsibility, self-assertiveness, purposeful living, and personal integrity to reach your full potential.

Psalm 139:14 - "I will praise You, for I am fearfully and wonderfully made; Marvelous are Your works, And that my soul knows very well."

1 Peter 2:9 But you are a chosen generation, a royal priesthood, a holy nation, His own special people, that you may proclaim the praises of Him who called you out of darkness into His marvelous light.

Ephesians 5:27 - that He might present her to Himself a glorious church, not having spot or wrinkle or any such thing, but that she should be holy and without blemish.

And a time to laugh

Genesis 18:12 Therefore Sarah laughed within herself, saying, "After I have grown old, shall I have pleasure, my lord being old also?" Genesis 21:6 And Sarah said, "God has made me laugh, and all who hear will laugh with me."

Job 8:21 He will yet fill your mouth with laughing, And your lips with rejoicing.

Psalm 126:2 - Then our mouth was filled with laughter, And our tongue with singing. Then they said among the nations, "The LORD has done great things for them."

Nehemiah 8:10 - ... for the joy of the LORD is your strength."

Psalm 32:11 - Be glad in the LORD and rejoice, you righteous; And shout for joy, all you upright in heart!

A Time to Dance

A time to embrace

A time to gain – Confidence

The differences between men's and women's brains show that women are more likely to worry than men. A loving husband will help his wife gain confidence.

Ladies understand that you are the one to build your confidence whether your husband helps or not. The scripture tells us to be strong, bold and of good courage. Ladies you are to rise above strife and doubt and ascend to strict confidence.

Deuteronomy 31:6 Be strong and of good courage, do not fear nor be afraid of them; for the LORD your God, He is the One who goes with you. He will not leave you nor forsake you."

Deuteronomy 31:7 Then Moses called Joshua and said to him in the sight of all Israel, "Be strong and of good courage, for you must go with this people to the land which the LORD has sworn to their fathers to give them, and you shall cause them to inherit it.

Deuteronomy 31:23 Then He inaugurated Joshua the son of Nun, and said, "Be strong and of good courage; for you shall bring the children of Israel into the land of which I swore to them, and I will be with you."

Joshua 1:6 Be strong and of good courage, for to this people you shall divide as an inheritance the land which I swore to their fathers to give them.

Joshua 1:9 Have I not commanded you? Be strong and of good courage; do not be afraid, nor be dismayed, for the LORD your God is with you wherever you go."

Joshua 1:18 Whoever rebels against your command and does not heed your words, in all that you command him, shall be put to death. Only be strong and of good courage."

Joshua 10:25 Then Joshua said to them, "Do not be afraid, nor be dismayed; be strong and of good courage, for thus the LORD will do to all your enemies against whom you fight."

2 Samuel 10:12 Be of good courage, and let us be strong for our people and for the cities of our God. And may the LORD do what is good in His sight."

1 Chronicles 19:13 Be of good courage, and let us be strong for our people and for the cities of our God. And may the LORD do what is good in His sight."

1 Chronicles 22:13 Then you will prosper, if you take care to fulfill the statutes and judgments with which the LORD charged Moses concerning Israel. Be strong and of good courage; do not fear nor be dismayed.

1 Chronicles 28:20 And David said to his son Solomon, "Be strong and of good courage, and do it; do not fear nor be dismayed, for the LORD God—my God—will be with you. He will not leave you nor forsake you, until you have finished all the work for the service of the house of the LORD.

Ezra 10:4 Arise, for this matter is your responsibility. We also are with you. Be of good courage and do it."

Psalm 27:14 - Wait on the LORD; Be of good courage, And He shall strengthen your heart; Wait, I say, on the LORD!

Psalm 31:24 - Be of good courage, And He shall strengthen your heart, All you who hope in the LORD.

Lack of self-confidence for female men is built upon worry and procrastination. Female men who tend to *ruminate* i.e. think carefully and deeply about something repeatedly rather than *act* are less likely to feel comfortable in new situations, relax when things don't go to plan and seize an opportunity as it arises. Self-confidence for female men, is the ability to face new challenges with optimism, walk into a room full of people with less-than-perfect make up, and still trust that a smile and a friendly manner will be what interests and engages others. Female men can learn Self-confidence, contrary to widespread belief that it isn't always bestowed at birth, it is learned.

Have you ever seen a child taking their first faltering steps? Despite falling, a thousand times, within a short space of time they are walking all over the place, then running, dancing and jumping. In the same way, we can build a set of skills that enable us to feel better about ourselves.

Female men are more prone to confidence-destroyers than men. Some nerves are natural for both genders, a new date or an important meeting with your boss will often cause a few feelings of anxiety, the trick is not to waste time negatively predicting the outcome. When you think that you don't look your best, maybe not had enough time to get ready or having put on a few pounds, it is easy to feel that everything else will go badly as a result. The sure thing is that if you dwell on that single thought you are not going to enjoy the event.

Female men tend to be more sensitive to others' needs, and more aware of changes that might improve a situation or make it more comfortable for someone. Unchecked however, this ability to think things over can turn into over-analysis and make life miserable as this internal process leads to confusion, anxiety and inaction.

Self-confidence in female men is attainable by having the ability to relax. When there is an event that naturally brings about a few butterflies, spend some time thinking about times that you have done well at something, remember what it is like to feel good, then take a few moments to imagine yourself with those feelings in the future.

Notice how your posture, facial gestures and words feel and sound, and what a difference it makes to the enjoyment of any event. If it is a meeting or public performance, remember that preparation and a belief in a positive outcome are key, even if we can't exactly predict the outcome we know that feeling relaxed releases the thinking part of the brain to get on with the job in hand to the best of our abilities.

Female men are more likely to read more into facial gestures and voice intonation which is a useful trait, however developing an optimistic attitude will increase your self-confidence.

1 Peter 4:8 - And above all things have fervent love for one another, for "love will cover a multitude of sins."

Therefore, before the adversaries of ifs, what's and maybes find their way into your thought patterns, work on developing the power of optimism to vanquish negative rumination and allow the possibility of composure.

Romans 8:28 And we know that all things work together for good to those who love God, to those who are the called according to His purpose.

Evidently, female men who appear confident have ability to notice that even if they are feeling a little nervous inside they take their attention to the world around them.

Philippians - 4:8 Finally, brethren, whatever things are true, whatever things are noble, whatever things are just, whatever things are pure, whatever things are lovely, whatever things are of good report, if there is any virtue and if there is anything praiseworthy—meditate on these things.

A Time to keep and a Time to throw away

Romans 12:9 - Let love be without hypocrisy. Abhor what is evil. Cling to what is good.

A time to keep silence

Psalm 31:18 Let the lying lips be put to silence, which speak insolent things proudly and contemptuously against the righteous.

And a time to speak and A time to love

Ezekiel 16:8 - "When I passed by you again and looked upon you, indeed our time was the time of love; so I spread My wing over you and covered your nakedness. Yes, I swore an oath to you and entered into a covenant with you, and you became Mine," says the Lord GOD.

And a Time to Hate

Romans 12:9 - Let love be without hypocrisy. Abhor what is evil.

Psalm 5:5 The boastful shall not stand in Your sight; You hate all workers of iniquity.

Psalm 9:13 Have mercy on me, O LORD! Consider my trouble from those who hate me, You who lift me up from the gates of death

A time of War

Exodus 15:3 - The LORD is a man of war; The LORD is His name.

2 Chronicles 20:15 ….. be not afraid nor dismayed by reason of this great multitudes; for the battle is not yours, but God's.

2 Chronicles 20:17 - You shall not need to fight in this battle: Set yourselves, stand ye still, and see the salvation of the Lord with you, …..

1 Timothy 6:12 – Fight the good fight of faith, lay hold on eternal life, to which you were also called and have confessed the good confession in the presence of many witnesses.

And a time of peace

Numbers 6:26 - *The* LORD *lift up His countenance upon you, And give you peace.*

Psalm 37:37 - *Mark the blameless man, and observe the upright; For the future of that man is peace.*

Proverbs 3:2 For length of days and long life and peace- they will add to you.

Proverbs 16:7 When a man's ways please the LORD, *He makes even his enemies to be at peace with him.*

Isaiah 26:3 You will keep him in perfect peace, Whose mind is stayed on You, Because he trusts in You.

Isaiah 54:13 All your children shall be taught by the LORD, *And great shall be the peace of your children.*

Matthew 5:9 Blessed are the peacemakers, for they shall be called sons of God.

Romans 16:20 And the God of peace will crush Satan under your feet shortly. The grace of our Lord Jesus Christ be with you.

Ephesians 4:3 endeavoring to keep the unity of the Spirit in the bond of peace.

Hebrews 12:14 Pursue peace with all people, and holiness, without which no one will see the Lord:

Jude 1:2 Mercy, peace, and love be multiplied to you.

1 Corinthians 7:3-5 [3] Let the husband render to his wife the affection due her, and likewise also the wife to her husband. [4] The

GOD'S ORDER AND PURPOSE OF MARRIAGE

wife does not have authority over her own body, but the husband does. And likewise, the husband does not have authority over his own body, but the wife does. ⁵Do not deprive one another except with consent for a time, that you may give yourselves to fasting and prayer; and come together again so that Satan does not tempt you because of your lack of self-control.). Nor are they to focus on their own pleasure but rather the giving of pleasure to their spouse.

This oneness and desire which is to benefit each other is not automatic, especially after mankind's fall into sin. The man, in (Genesis 2:24 (KJV) ²⁴Therefore a man shall leave his father and mother and be joined to his wife, and they shall become one flesh.), is told to "cleave" to his wife. This word has two ideas behind it. One is to be "glued" to his wife, a picture of how tight the marriage bond is to be adhesive and bound. The other aspect is to "pursue hard after" the wife. This "pursuing hard after" is to go beyond the courtship leading to marriage and is to continue throughout the marriage. The fleshly tendency or attitude is to "do what feels good to me" rather than to consider what will benefit the spouse. And this self-centeredness egocentric attitude is the RUT or routine that marriages commonly fall into once the "honeymoon is over." Instead of each spouse dwelling upon how his or her own needs are not being met, he or she is to remain focused on meeting the needs of the spouse. As nice as it may be for two people to live together meeting each other's needs, God has a higher calling for the marriage. Even as they were to be serving Christ with their lives before marriage

Romans 12:1-2 - I beseech you therefore, brethren, by the mercies of God, that you present your bodies a living sacrifice, holy, acceptable to God, which is your reasonable service. ²And do not be conformed to this world, but be transformed by the renewing of your mind, that you may prove what is that good and acceptable and perfect will of God.), now they are to serve Christ together as a unit and raise their children to serve God

1 Corinthians 7:29-34 - ³²But I want you to be without care. He who is unmarried cares for the things of the Lord—how he may please the Lord. ³³ But he who is married cares about the things of the world—how he may please his wife. ³⁴ There is a difference between a wife and a virgin. The unmarried woman cares about the things of the Lord, that she may be holy both in body and in spirit. But she who is married cares about the things of the world—how she may please her husband; Malachi 2:15 But did He not make them one, Having a remnant of the Spirit? And why one? He seeks godly offspring. Therefore take heed to your spirit, And let none deal treacherously with the wife of his youth; (Ephesians 6:4 ⁴And you, fathers, do not provoke your children to wrath, but bring them up in the training and admonition of the Lord.

Priscilla and Aquila, in Acts 18, would be good examples of this. As a couple pursues serving Christ together, the joy which the Spirit gives will fill their marriage and they became strong in their relationship Galatians 5:22-23.

In the Garden of Eden, there were three present: Adam, Eve, and God, and there was joy. So, if God is central in a marriage today, there also will be joy. Without God, a true and full oneness is not possible.

Chapter 9

Marriage Models

Examples or models of godly Marriage relationship between a man and a woman are found in the scripture.

First, Marriage between a male man and a female man is to reflect the relationship that exists between The Father and the Son

Second, Marriage between a male man and a female man is to reflect the relationship that exists between Christ and the Church.

Third, Marriage _ Christ and the Church Relationship

Ephesians 5:22-33 (NKJV) ²²Wives, submit to your own husbands, as to the Lord. ²³For the husband is head of the wife, as also Christ is head of the church; and He is the Savior of the body. ²⁴Therefore, just as the church is subject to Christ, so let the wives be to their own husbands in everything. ²⁵Husbands, love your wives, just as Christ also loved the church and gave Himself for her, ²⁶that He might sanctify and cleanse her with the washing of water by the word, ²⁷that He might present her to Himself a glorious church, not having spot or wrinkle or any such thing, but that she should be holy and without blemish. ²⁸So husbands ought to love their own wives as their own bodies; he who loves his wife loves himself. ²⁹For no one ever hated his own flesh, but nourishes and cherishes it, just as the Lord does the church. ³⁰For we are members of His body, of His flesh and of

His bones. ³¹"For this reason a man shall leave his father and mother and be joined to his wife, and the two shall become one flesh." ³²This is a great mystery, but I speak concerning Christ and the church. ³³Nevertheless let each one of you in particular so love his own wife as himself, and let the wife see that she respects her husband.

Christ and the church relationship is the model of Husband and wife relationship. The specific instructions Paul gives for husband and wife is a glimpse of the BRIDEGROOM and BRIDE. Bridegroom and Bride is a heavenly model for every marriage on earth.

Proverbs 18:22 ²²Whoso finds a wife finds a good thing and obtains favor of the LORD.

A wife is a treasure. She is a jewel, husband's world, his sunshine, a gift from The Lord and through her he obtains favor with The Lord.

Please read what the scriptures says in **James 1:17 Every good gift and every perfect gift is from above, and comes down from the Father of lights, with whom there is no variation or shadow of turning.**

If then a God chosen wife to the husband is a good thing, a gift, a blessing and brings the husband favor from the Lord, my million-dollar question to you who deal with your wives treacherously is, when did she become dreadful, evil, and worthless to you to make her a sex object, a victim of your hatred, rage, abuse and oppression? When did God start giving undesirable things to be subjected to atrocity? When did a good thing from God become so horrendous to inflict pain and hurt on her? Your wife is a blessing and gift to you from God.

The scripture in Proverbs 10:22 says that **"The blessing of the LORD makes one rich, And He adds no sorrow with it"**

Proverbs 19:14 ¹⁴House and riches are the inheritance of fathers: and a prudent wife is from the LORD.

Chapter 10

Headship

Headship means Stewardship. It means the careful and responsible management of something entrusted to one's care.

Husband (male man) Is Head of the Wife (Female man)

In the Christian culture when the Bible was written, there was a generalization advocating government in which power is shared which we would be referred to "Federal Headship." This means that the male is the one who represents his descendants. Confirmation of this is in *Heb. 7:8-10.* - **"And in this case mortal men receive tithes, but in that case, one receives them, of whom it is witnessed that he lives on. ⁹ And, so to speak, through Abraham even Levi, who received tithes, paid tithes, ¹⁰ for he was still in the loins of his father when Melchizedek met him."**

Notice that it says that Levi paid tithes while still in the loins of his father Abraham. How did he do this? By proxy since Abraham, his distant "father" represented him.

Likewise, we see the concept of Federal Headship in the fall. It was Eve who first sinned. But sin entered the world through Adam - not **through Eve.**

Romans 5:12 says, "Therefore, just as through one man sin entered into the world, and death through sin, and so death spread to all men, because all sinned."

This is because Adam represented humanity and creation. When Adam fell, we fell. This is the reason why the bible says, in *1 Cor. 15:22* " . . . *in Adam all die.*" Also, the bible says in *Romans 5:15* *"For if by the transgression of the one [Adam] many died, much more did the grace of God and the gift by the grace of the one Man, Jesus Christ, abound to the many."*

This brings us to the woman (female man). Notice that it says in **Genesis 2:24, "For this cause a man shall leave his father and his mother, and shall cleave to his wife; and they shall become one flesh."**

When **a male** man and a **female** man are joint by God in marriage, they become on flesh. There is a unity between them. But, it is the male man who is the leader of the family which is why it says that the male man is the head of the female man.

Some may think that this was a cultural notion that **sneaked** into the Bible. But Paul makes it clear that the headship is related to the created order:

1 Cor. 11:8-10 For man does not originate from woman, but woman from man; ⁹ for indeed man was not created for the woman's sake, but woman for the man's sake. ¹⁰ Therefore the woman ought to have a symbol of authority on her head, because of the angels."

It was because Eve listened to the devil that the issue of order and hierarchy in the marriage relationship has had to be raised and explained.

Genesis 3:16 - I will greatly multiply your pain in childbirth. In pain you shall bring forth children; yet your desire shall be for your husband, and he shall rule over you."

This headship is not about having the upper hand, nor is it to mean that a woman has no rights or is a second-class citizen. On the contrary, God tells the husband some very serious commands:

Ephesians 5:25-27 - Husbands, love your wives, just as Christ also loved the church and gave Himself up for her; [26] that He might sanctify her, having cleansed her by the washing of water with the Word, [27] that He might present to Himself the church in all her glory, having no spot or wrinkle or any such thing; but that she should be holy and blameless."

Finally, the headship issue is an issue of order--not of who is better or more important. The husband is the head of the wife in the family, and he has the responsibility of guiding his family to a closer relationship with the Lord. God will require it of him on the day when all our deeds are judged by God.

1 Corinthians 11:3 - "But I want you to know that the head of every man is Christ, the head of woman is man, and the head of Christ is God."

The head here implies stewardship, leadership and guidance.

- a) God is the head of Christ
- b) Christ is the head of the church
- c) Male Man is the head of the female man

1. Father Son Relationship is a model the scripture gives for marriage between **a male** man and a **female** man. The relationship between God as The Head and Christ as son is given as a model for the relationship between husband and wife.

When the Bible reveals how The Father and Son relate to each other, it tells us the way husband and wife are to relate to each other. Husband and wife are to share a mutual love like God and Christ do.

John 5:20 - For the Father loves the Son, and shows Him all things that He Himself does; and He will show Him greater works than these, that you may marvel.

John 14:31 states that "But that the world may know that I love the Father, and as The Father gave Me commandment, so I do. Arise, let us go from here."

When it comes to stewardship a husband is to have ability of unusual decisiveness to tell his bride every time "let us go from here." He is to acquire leadership acumen to be able to tell his wife every time *"let us go from here."*

Chapter 11

Husband Role In Marriage

Leadership in the home is not a self-complacency matter. The biblical meaning and responsibilities of husband and wife in the home has been redefined by the culture that is defiant of their Creator. Many male men are confused and insecure. They do not know how to act in their home and most of it is to be blamed on their upbringing. They lacked a good model for leadership at home and have no mental picture of what it means to steward a family. Consequently, they do not lead effectively, or they do not even try.

Increasingly, many male men are becoming passive in the home. They have decided that the easiest thing to do is to do nothing. The simplest thing with the smallest risk is to stay on the fence with both feet firmly planted in mid-air and let the female man (wife) do it. When a male man is married to a strong female man (wife) who will take over, he often lets her do just that.

The Scriptures clearly give us the servant/head model for being a male man, a husband and father.

I pray that the concepts I share here will help you understand the biblical role of a husband more clearly than ever before. When the biblical meaning and responsibilities of husband and wife in the home are correctly interpreted, and applied, they not only result in freedom for the husband and wife, but also help you work better as a team (together each achieves more) to combat isolation and conflict in your marriage.

Three responsibilities flow out of proper leadership.

The first responsibility for a husband you are to **Be a leader to your wife and family.** The Scriptures provide a clear and profound organizational structure for a marriage.

God placed ultimate responsibility with respect to the household on the shoulders of the husband. The Lord has assigned the wife the duty of obeying her husband in the Lord, yet this obedience must be a voluntary submission on her part, and that only to her own husband, not to every man."

"Head" does not mean male dominance, where a man lords it over to the female man and demands her total obedience to his every wish and command. God never viewed female man (women) inferior to male man (man) or as second-class citizens. His Word clearly states that we are all equally His children and are of equal value and worth before Him. *Galatians 3:28 tells us, "There is neither Jew nor Greek, slave nor free, male nor* **female, for you are all one in Christ Jesus"**

The New Testament teachings profoundly and clearly shows that female man (women) are to be respected, revered, and treated as equals with male men (men). Unfortunately, many husbands have not gotten the message. They degrade their wives by neglect or with insensitive and abusive treatment. Male men (Men) abandoned God's design of leadership. When God presented Eve to Adam in the Garden, Adam received her as a gift of immense value to God and him. When husbands, particularly Christian husbands, do not treat their wives as a precious gift from God and helpmate, they can cause those wives to search for a way to find significance and value as persons, often outside God's will.

GOD'S ORDER AND PURPOSE OF MARRIAGE

To recapture God's design for marriage men will have to know how to take over, have things under control, guide, and get things done. It is not about being strong or being born natural leaders, but taking responsibility. God has equipped the husband with leadership gift to lead. He has placed it inside the husband. They simply need to take carriage and just develop the gift in them and it shall make room for them.

The apostle Paul wrote to Timothy, 2 **Timothy 1:5-7 ⁵when I call to remembrance the genuine faith that is in you, which dwelt first in your grandmother Lois and your mother Eunice, and I am persuaded is in you also. ⁶Therefore I remind you to stir up the gift of God which is in you through the laying on of my hands. ⁷For God has not given us a spirit of fear, but of power and of love and of a sound mind.**

The gift is in you men, but you have the responsibility of stirring it up. The gift is not something we learn. It is something God gave us. It is something we need to discover and then stir up. No one else can activate your gift for you. You must do it yourself. You stir up your gift by developing, refining, enhancing, and using it.

Education can't give you your gift, but it can help you develop it so that it can be used to the maximum.

Proverbs 17:8 NKJV) says, "A gift is as a precious stone in the eyes of its possessor; wherever he turns, he prospers"

In other words, a gift is like a precious stone to the one who has it, and whenever he stirs it up, it turns into prosperity.

Men, you are encouraged to use your gift, it will prosper your marriage, family, vocation, business and assignment. Many people are working for money. That's an inferior reason to work. We must work for God's purpose within us. We work to get a seed to sow so it can be multiplied and come to us as a harvest.

Proverbs 18:16 ^{16}A man's gift makes room for him, and brings him before great men.

God does not tell you to do anything that He has not equipped you for. That is why the bible says in **"Philippians 4:13 - I can do all things through Christ who strengthens me." It also says in 2 Timothy 1:6 - Therefore I remind you to stir up the gift of God which is in you through the laying on of my hands.**

God has placed the husband in the position of responsibility. It does not matter what kind of personality a man may have. Your wife may be resisting you, fighting you, and spurning your attempts to lead, but it makes no difference. I believe our wives want us and need us to lead. You are not demanding this position; on the contrary, God placed you there. You will not lead her perfectly, but you must care for your wife and family by serving them with perseverance.

The scripture does more than assign leadership in a marriage to the husband. It provides a model for that leadership. The Apostle Paul says **1 Corinthians 11:3 that the husband is head of the wife as Christ is head of the church. "This comparison of the husband with Christ reveals the sense in which a man should be his wife's "head." He is her head as being vitally interested in her welfare. He is her protector.** His pattern is Christ Who, as head of the Church, is its Savior.

The second responsibility for a husband is to Love your wife unconditionally. Apostle Paul writing to husbands of Ephesus church admonished them saying,

Ephesians 5:25 "Husbands, love your wives, just as Christ also loved the church and gave Himself up for her."

Your unconditional acceptance of your wife is not based upon her performance, but on her worth as God's gift to you. If you want to love your wife unconditionally, always be sure her emotional tank is full. One of the best ways to do that is to affirm her constantly. Let her know verbally that you value her, respect her, and love her. You will very soon discover that you simply cannot do that enough.

Chapter 12

Your Wife Your Friend

lasting relationships come down to friendship. Lasting friendship is characterized by kindness, generosity, joy, and love that will carry the friends forward to their final days on this earth. There are three types of friends that God recognizes; an intimate friend, a covenant friend, and a prophetic friend, and are characterized by the three side of love; Agape love, Phileo love and Eros love.

An intimate friend is someone to whom private matters are confided. It is someone associated with close personal relations very private, closely personal, and warmly cozy, close personal connection experience. It is someone with an engagement characterized by Eros love relations. Our most intimate friend is not he or she we show our worst, but the best of our nature. Happiness and intimate friendship is the rainbow between two hearts sharing seven colors; Love, sadness, happiness, truth, faith, trust and respect.

To some men, a wife is an intimate friend only. To others she is both an intimate friend and a covenant friend. To others she is the three of them; intimate friend, covenant friend, and prophetic friend. Still to others she is none of these. She is a bed partner to warm up for him whenever he pleases and is convenient to him. Husbands, you must infuse your wife's being through and through as an intimate friend must always do so when you speak you speak of only her, and when you are silent you yearn for her. Husband, let your wife know that if you could catch a rainbow you would do it for her and share with her its beauty in the days she is feeling blue. If you could take her troubles, you would toss them into the sea. But since these things are impossible you are going to be what you know best; a friend that is always there for her. Let her know she is the one you prefer and hold dear. You both slipped briskly into an intimacy from which you will never recover. Affirm to her your love for her is perfect and without fear.

1 John 4:18 There is no fear in love; but perfect love casts out fear, because fear involves torment. But he who fears has not been made perfect in love.

Verbally and in deed confirm to her that you love her without fear, trust her without questioning, need her without demanding, want her without restrictions, accept her without change, and desire her without inhibitions. Before you can be friends with your wife you must first be friendly. Who is a friend? What does it really mean to be a friend to your wife? Have you ever seriously considered what it means to be friends with your wife? A friend is a confidant. A friend is someone you know well and regard with affection and trust. Is an associate who provides cooperation or assistance. A believer, an ally, an admirer. To be friendly means - Easy to understand or use. Inclined to help or support. Mutual trust and friendship among people spending a lot of time together. A friend is another term for comrade.

Scriptural meaning of the term "friend" is somewhat intimate and conveys a sense of closeness, trust, and sharing. "Proverbs 17:17 A friend loves at all times…."

Husband you are always to be a loving friend to your wife. True friendship and love coexist to complement each other. Where one is the other is there.

"Proverbs 18:22 & 24 - **He who finds a wife finds a good thing and obtains favor from the LORD. ²⁴A man who has friends must**

himself be friendly, but there is a friend who sticks closer than a brother."

The statement "he who finds a wife finds a good thing and obtains favor from the LORD" means that your wife is a gift and blessing from God to you. A wife that is sent to you from God is a good gift. Anything that comes from God is good and can never be bad or a curse. Those who do not come from God can be anything else other than good gift. Husband is to consider his wife good and the best gift ever from Jehovah.

"1 Peter3:7-9(NIV) ⁷Husbands, in the same way, treat your wives with consideration as a delicate vessel, and with honor as fellow heirs of the gracious gift of life, so that your prayers will not be hindered. ⁸Finally, all of you, be like-minded and sympathetic, love as brothers, be tender-hearted and humble ⁹Do not repay evil with evil or insult with insult, but with blessing, because to this you were called so that you may inherit a blessing."

Notice what verse 7 says! Husbands, ...treat your wives with consideration as (like) **a delicate vessel, not weaker vessel,** but easily hurt emotionally and with honor as fellow heirs of the gracious gift of life. A Wife is not weaker than her husband. God expects husband to nurture his wife like you would a new born babe, and a jewel because she is precious and a treasure. Both of you are equal heirs of the gracious gift of life. If you don't treat your wife right, you cannot inherit the gracious gift of life alone. It is meant for both of you. Both of you are to be like-minded and sympathetic, best friends and lovers of each other, tender-hearted and humble. **⁹Do** not repay evil with evil or insult with insult, but with blessing, because to this you were called so that you may inherit empowerment to prosper (blessing).

The friend referred to in Proverbs 18:24, who sticks closer than a brother does is the wife. The husband must invite her to friendship. He must himself be friendly to her to befriend her. In other words, make yourself the kind of friend you are supposed to become to your wife because you must first be friendly yourself.

It is the husband's job to bring the wife to his side and make her feel good about being her. Affirm her best qualities especially when she is feeling insecure. Call out the best in her and hold her accountable to the best version of herself. Listen to her without judging or trying to fix her. Give her the benefit of the doubt. Extend grace to her when she is grumpy or having a dreadful day. Remember her birthday, favorite foods, music, and places she likes. Know her story and love her regardless. Spend quality time with her, just because you enjoy her company. Speak well of her always, when she is present and when she is not present. Serve her with a joyful spirit and without complaining. Speak the truth to her when no one else will. Never shame her, diminish her, demean her, or make her feel small. Become excited about what she is excited about. Celebrate her wins!

James 2:3, 6 - 9 The kind of closeness with God that our hearts long for is only experienced by a few people. In the scripture, we see only a handful of people seemed to have a special relationship with the Father. In the same way, the kind of closeness with husbands that their wives' hearts long for is only experienced by a few wives. Abraham was called a friend of God. The Lord spoke with Moses face to face. Isaiah saw the Lord sitting on a throne. Paul was taken up into the third heaven, and the Apostle John had an incredible vision, which he recorded in the book of Revelation. We find a spiritual depth of communion with God and writers of terrific books that influence people's way of thinking, speaking and acting; and great hymns that not many of us experience. Is this special communion with the Lord reserved for a favored few? Is it presumptuous to consider that God, Himself, would be our intimate Friend? No! intimate Friend with God is for everybody and so it should for every couple who God joint. God is equitable and **gives** to all **liberally** whatever we ask in faith. **James 1:5 records - If any of you lacks wisdom, let him ask of God,** *who gives to all liberally* **and without reproach, and it will be given to him.**

The opportunity is open to all, however only a few find it. It is for those who decide to seek for it. Love is a decision you make to love, joy is a decision you make to rejoice, peace is a decision you make to be at peace, longsuffering is a decision you make to be at peace, kindness is a decision you make to be kind, goodness is a decision you make to be good, faithfulness is a decision you make to be faithful, gentleness is a decision you make to be gentle, self-control is a decision you make to be in control of situations and circumstances. Think of the possibilities if you focused this effort on your wife! Those *who are* Christ's decide to crucify the flesh with its passions and desires live in the Spirit, and walk in the Spirit. Conceited husbands provoke their wives to anger and distaste.

Your Wife Your Love Your Friend

Now that we know a wife as the friend that sticks closer to a husband than a brother, husband's love for his wife is to be greater enough to lay down his life for his best friend – the wife. Jesus exemplified this by laying down His life for sinners and called them His friends.

John 15:13 - Greater love has no one than this, than to lay down one's life for his friends.

By this we know love means that husbands ought to love their wives by laying down their lives for them. lasting relationships come down to friendship. Husbands must make an intentional effort to connect, share interests, and meet their wives' emotional needs.

1 John 3:16 By this we know love, because He laid down His life for us. And we also ought to lay down our lives for the brethren.

Mark 10:45 - For even the Son of Man came not to be served but to serve, and to give his life as a ransom for many.

Unlike English, in which the word *love* means many different things, Ancient Greek had four words to describe the range of meaning that our word *love* conveys.

The first word is *Eros*, from which we get the English word *erotic (desire for, to want, to or wish for something.)* Eros was the word often used to express sexual love or the feelings of arousal that are shared between husband and wife who are physically attracted to each other. The word was also used as the name of the Greek god of love, Eros. The Romans called him "Cupid. By New Testament times, this word had become so debased or corrupted by the culture that it is not used even once in the entire New Testament. Eros love is unique and delicious because it involves our **passions**. The Greek word Eros is the root word for the English word erotic and eroticism. This kind of love involves our hormones, chemistry, and sexual tension. When we feel attracted to someone it is because of the erotic part of love. We can feel this for more than one person over our life time. When we are young we sometimes refer to this as puppy love. When we are older we say that we are "in love" with that person. You can fall in love and out of love with the same person which makes Eros a very confusing and mysterious kind of love that cannot be trusted.

The book of "Song of Solomon" in the Bible sometimes called "The Song of Songs is devoted entirely to Eros love. It is fitting so entitled because erotic love is so intoxicating that it represents one of the most pleasurable experiences we have on earth. Certainly, most of our popular songs and romantic movies are written filled with words and images that idolize this side of love. This creates a misconception in our society that Eros love is the purest form of love. This leaves the illusion that it is the only kind of love that exists. I am persuaded that when people talk about finding their soul-mate that is what they mean. It is as if, when you are in love, the whole universe opens up and the two of you are united as one person.

Also, in today's world, if you lose the feelings of passion for your partner, this is often an acceptable reason for ending a marriage. It is as if we should change our marriage vows to say that I will stay with you as long as I stay "in love" with you. Our society makes the mistake of forgetting about the equal importance of the other 2 sides of love.

Eros love is centered on *feelings*. Those born of the Spirit of God walk by faith not by sensory. They don't get intimate to gratify their fleshly appetite, but to enrich their marriage relationship. Remember that sex is a gift and a blessing from God and He says His gifts/blessings make us rich without adding sorrow with them. It is a privilege not a right.

Christians' marriage relationship cannot be established and build on Eros love for the following reasons. The first is that feelings are not thought of or spoken highly of in our Christian subculture. The second reason is that feelings can change so rapidly. The third reason is that feelings are mystical, illusive, not concrete or black and white, hard to be in-touch with, and overall hard to trust. It is for these reasons that we relegate Eros as less important than Agape and Phileo love. In the end, the world overemphasizes and idealizes Eros love while the church compensates by overemphasizing and idealizing agape love. A balance toward all three is more balanced, makes more sense, and is healthier.

On a personal note, I love the Eros side of love and am so thankful to God that He included this in His creation. I am also part of the population that fell in love at first sight. I am a romantic at heart and, therefore, have a natural draw to Eros. I have told my children that it would be a mistake to marry someone with whom they are not attracted. It seems so basic and simple, but if we were to take the church's over-compensating teachings about love to the logical extreme, it would be as if we would be able to be married to anyone. This is because if we take Eros love out of the equation and say that agape love is superior and the one we can trust, then it's logically sound that we can unconditionally love anyone for marriage. In His amazing wisdom, God has given all three sides of love to make a good and healthy marriage.

The second Greek word for "love" was *Storge*, which referred to natural, familial love. *Storge* (a word not found in the Bible) referred to the type of love shown by a parent for a child.

The third Greek word for "love" was *Phileo*, which forms part of the words *philosophy* ("love of wisdom") and *philanthropy* ("love of fellow man"). This word speaks of the warm affection shared between friends. Whereas *Eros* is more closely associated with the libido, *Phileo* is associated with the heart (metaphorically speaking). We feel love for our friends and family, obviously not in an erotic sense, but in the sense of being kind and affectionate. However, *Phileo* is not felt between people who are at enmity with one another. We can feel *Phileo* toward friends and family, but not toward people whom we dislike or hate.

The fourth Greek word for "love," is *Agapé*, typically defined as the "self-sacrificing love." This is the love that moves people into action and looks out for the well-being of others, no matter the personal cost. Biblically speaking, *Agapé* is the love God showed to His people in sending His Son, Jesus, to die for their sins. It is the love that focuses on the will, not the emotions, experience, or libido. This is the love that Jesus commands His disciples to show toward their enemies (Luke 6:35). *Eros* and *Phileo* are not expressed to people who hate us and wish us ill; *Agapé* is. In Romans 5:8, Paul tells us that God's love for His people was made manifest in that "while we were still sinners i.e., enemies, Christ died for us."

Therefore, moving from the base to the pure, we have *Eros*, *Storge*, *Phileo*, and *Agapé*. This is not to denigrate or play down *Eros* as sinful or impure. Sexual love is not inherently unclean or evil. Rather, it is the gift of God to married couples to express their love for one another, strengthen the bond between them, and ensure the survival of humanity. It should not be abused, forced, demanded, but consensual. It has been misconstrued, misapplied, by traditions and religious dogmatic dominance to oppress the female man. The Bible devotes Song of Solomon to the blessings of erotic, or sexual, love. The love between a husband and a wife should be, among other things, an erotic love. However, a long-term relationship based solely on *Eros* is doomed to failure. The "thrill" of sexual love wears off quickly unless there are some Storge, *Phileo* and *Agapé* to go along with it.

Even though there is nothing inherently sinful with erotic love, it is in this sphere that our sinful nature is easily made manifest because *Eros* focuses primarily on sensuality and self. *Storge, Phileo*, and *agapé* focus on relationship with others. Consider what the apostle Paul tells the Colossian church in "Colossians 3:5 Put to death therefore what is earthly in you: sexual immorality, impurity, passion, evil desire, and covetousness, which is idolatry".

The Greek word for "sexual immorality" is *Porneia* (the root of our word *pornography*). This essentially covers the complete extend or range of sexual sin (adultery, fornication, homosexuality, bestiality, lesbianism, incest, hedonistic, incestuous).

When shared between husband and wife, erotic love can be a wonderful thing, but because of our fallen sin nature, expressions of *Eros* too often become *Porneia*. In dealing with *Eros*, human beings tend to go to extremes, becoming either ascetics or hedonists. The ascetic completely eschews sensual or sexual love. The hedonist sees unrestrained sexual passion and all forms of sensuality as perfectly natural and to be indulged. The biblical view is a balance between these two sinful extremes. Within the bond of heterosexual marriage, God celebrates the beauty of sexual love: "Let my lover come into his garden and taste its choice fruits. I have come into my garden, my sister, my bride; I have gathered my myrrh with my spice. I have eaten my honeycomb and my honey; I have drunk my wine and my milk. Eat, O friends, and drink; drink your fill, O lovers" Song of Solomon 4:16—5:1. Outside of biblical marriage, *Eros* becomes distorted and sinful.

Many women have presented me with major problem that they were no longer "in love" with their husbands. They have stated that they loved their husbands, but that the husbands were seeing other women. When they realized their husbands were unfaithful they no longer had the feelings of passion for them anymore. They have told me that they were beginning to wonder if they had, in fact, ever been "in love" with their husbands. They said they were Christian and they knew what the right thing was to do, but no matter how much they tried and how much they prayed, their feelings continued to wane for their husbands.

These women's problem is more common, even in our churches, than we want to admit. By understanding love more fully, some have been able to make more choices than the knew they had. The more you understand and appreciate the 3 sides of love the more you will be able to love the significant people God has put into your life more fully.

The problem with partial teaching of love is that it presents only part of the truth. The Bible teaches through the Greek language that love has 3 sides or parts to it. In the English language we only have one word for love. In Greek, love is given the names of **Agape**, **Phileo**, and **Eros**. By understanding the meaning of these different names for love, we can better understand what love is, we can evaluate our present love relationship, and we can take steps to improve our marriages.

Each form of love is equally as important as the others. By seeing love as more expanded through the Greek language, culture, and view, we begin to appreciate love as more than just a choice and, more than just a feeling.

Agape love

Agape love is committed love. Depending on the amount of commitment, this kind of love becomes increasingly unconditional. If the commitment is ultimate and infinite, such as the kind of love that God has for us, this love becomes completely unconditional. In other words, once we become children of God, His unconditional love is not diminished by our sin. He may become disappointed with us, but His steadfast agape love is unwavering "I will never leave you or forsake you **Hebrews 13:5**". This kind of love is not moved by circumstances such as the loss of youthful beauty, the loss of money, or health. Our marital vows say "for better or worse," "for richer or for poorer," "in sickness and in health," and "until death do us part." If we see it from this perspective, our marital vows are a covenant not a contract.

Agape love is also ruled by our will. When I say love is in the mind I mean "love is a choice. What I am telling you, is that you choose to love. Other times I have heard sermons that state that agape love is the way that God loves us, and this is also true. But this is also the partial truth, because God also loves us with the kind of love that the other two Greek words represent.

Sometimes I like to say that agape love is best represented by our hands. This is because it is our *will* that what tells our *hands* what to do. In a relationship that is long-term, like marriage, agape love is necessary because the commitment keeps the relationship together, especially when the going gets tough. It keeps solidarity in our marriages by giving both partners the security they need to make it when the storms, that are a natural part of any long-term relationship, seem to want to rip away the very fabric and foundation of our marriages. Even in the face of some very difficult conflicts and seemingly irreconcilable differences, agape love stays the course through the commitment of our will telling our hands to hang in there. Therefore, **Agape Love is** commitment, unconditional, choice, our will, our hands.

Phileo Love

Phileo love is best described as the kind of love that you would have for a friend or a sibling, such as a brother. When we incorporate this idea of brotherly love into a marriage relationship, we are suggesting that it is important for you to become best friends with your spouse. This means building bridges of common interest. These could be shared behaviors and activities or shared interests in the world of ideas and thoughts. Enduring friendships last because of trust and the sheer pleasure derived from sharing certain pleasurable experiences. This could mean such things as the joy that comes from raising children and building a home together, going to museums, playing sports, hiking, music, laughter, and going out to dinner, to name a few.

Some couples make the mistake of taking their friendship for granted or are misguided by the misconception that friendships should just happen. They assume that good friends shouldn't have to work at it to make it happen. It is easy to get yourself into trouble if your primary and closest friends are either your family, other friends (even of the same gender), or co-workers with whom you may share your most intimate thoughts and feelings. This kind of friendship needs to be nurtured and guarded by being granted only to your spouse.

If marriage relationship is going to last husband and wife should begin to appreciate the interrelatedness of the 3 sides of love. Once a friendship has been started in God, it is the couples' responsibility to intentionally give themselves wholly to it. This intentionality involves your **will** by deciding to make it a priority and through the **commitment** to establish these bridges no matter how far away you may feel from each other. This means that agape love helps foster better phileo love by committing to building and nurturing bridges of friendship.

In my marriage, this becomes a reality by Jedidah and my willingness to take seriously what kinds of things we can do for and with each other that make us happy. If these things make us both happy, then this is ideal. We both end up with a smile on our faces and with the reality that we made a good memory, no matter how big or small. These things may include going out to dinner, having friends and family over for dinner, walking together, reading, going to the beach, traveling, connecting at the end of the day, and sharing things with each other that we don't say to other people.

Sometimes we compromise by doing things that are of interest to the other person. For me, this means I must be willing to go the mall, spend time with my wife's family when I would rather be relaxing in my own backyard, do business projects because they are important to her. For my wife Jedidah, it means staying up later than she would want to, talking through and trying to resolve areas of conflict when it is more in her nature to let things slide, going to women breakfast gatherings and spending time playing at all kinds of things.

Phileo love includes what we are ***thinking*** or what is in our ***mind***. For instance, if agape love involves how our will directs our hands, phileo love involves how our thoughts direct our thinking. This means when we love someone with phileo love we are connecting with them on a mind level. Just remember how good you have felt when you have had a great talk with one of your best friends or have done something that was spontaneously funny that only the two of you would do and understand. These are the kinds of things husband and wife who are best friends do. They put their arms around each other and laugh into the night. Additionally, a best friend is there when you need them the most, and they accept you unconditionally when you are embarrassed about making a mistake or when you are not looking your best. They are willing to talk about anything, no matter how hard. They share with you things that you are even afraid to say to God, and they understand and want to understand.

God loves us with phileo love. We know this by the fact that in Isaiah God calls Abraham his friend *Isaiah 41:8 "But you, Israel, are My servant, Jacob whom I have chosen, The descendants of **Abraham** My friend.) God* did this after Abraham walked before Him all his life in righteousness. (**Genesis 48:15(b)** - And he blessed Joseph, and said: "**God**, before whom my fathers **Abraham** and Isaac **walked**)

In the Gospel of John, Jesus Christ called the disciples his friends. He did this after spending nearly three years with them teaching them all they needed to know. This must have meant a great deal to them to be called a friend by the Lord Jesus. If God in Jesus called human beings his friends, God must feel the same way towards us. And since He called us into relationship with Him, part of His plan must be that He loves us in a phileo kind of way. Man was created with God's attributes, with phileo love. Phileo love is real practical and lasts. It cannot be faked. It is the most intense love Husband and wife can experience.

In summary, ideal marriages have equally high amounts of each of these three sides of love. Marriages start to suffer when one or more of these are compromised. No marriage lives up to the ideal, all the time. If your marriage is suffering in one of these areas, this comparison can give you a frame of reference as to where you should be putting your energies. Also, the three sides of love are interrelated and affect each other. Therefore, for example, if you want more Eros you can increase this by being more committed to the relationship and by seeking a better friendship by taking your communication level deeper. Finally, it is important to realize and appreciate that God gave us all three, that He considers them all to be equally important, that He loves us unconditionally, calls us His friend, and that He is deeply passionate about us. I can't think of better news!

Love is a gentle caring and quiet concern deeply hidden in the heart. A presence always felt every day, every hour and every minute. Love is a gentle embrace between body, soul and spirit. A quiet touch of the hand, a soft hug by warm harms a caress of two souls. Love is a great passion between hungry hearts. The intimate exchange between Spirit, soul and body.

Chapter 13

Endearing Friendship

God is the initiator of intimacy. Intimacy is close or confidential friendship. Rather than making it mysterious or unobtainable, God has *sought* that kind of relationship with us from the beginning: "Let us make man in our image, in our likeness"

(Gen. 1:26 (NKJV) [26] Then God said, "Let Us make man in Our image, according to Our likeness; let them have dominion over the fish of the sea, over the birds of the air, and over the cattle, over all[a] the earth and over every creeping thing that creeps on the earth.").

He revealed Himself to the patriarchs and prophets; He personally led the Israelites in the wilderness by cloud and by fire. God's ultimate invitation to fellowship with us was in sending His Son to pay the price for our sin so that we who believe could be called His children. To seal His presence in us, He sent His Holy Spirit to dwell within us.

God continually invites us to respond to His love and desire for fellowship. He longs to love us as only He can, and He wants us to know Him in all of His fullness. His commandment to us is "Love the LORD your God with all your heart and with all your soul and with all your strength" (Deuteronomy. 6:5). He *wants* us to be intimate with Him. Why, then, only a few of us experience the kind of love relationship with God that He describes in the scripture? What does it take to know God as an intimate Friend? We can know God as an intimate Friend by expressing the longing, the honesty, the depth of feeling the psalmists expressed to Him. This is how God wants us to fellowship with Him and our fellow mates, and to grow in intimacy with Him and our mates. Learning the hearts of the psalmists, we can deepen our understanding of what friendship with God is like and of how it is developed and the apply the same to our marriage relationships.

Profound Passion

Saints who have enjoyed exceptional closeness with God have deeply longed for it. God promised in Jeremiah. 29:13: "You will seek me and find me when you seek me with all your heart."

Longing for God must be inextinguishable. Even when we are pursued by enemies, we do not only seek deliverance or a change in circumstances, but we seek God. Husbands and wives who have enjoyed exceptional closeness with each other have deeply longed for it. Longing for each other must be insatiable or inextinguishable. Even when pursued by enemies, couples who God joint will not only seek a change in circumstances, but will seek each other.

In Psalm 63:1 David records, "O God, you are my God, earnestly I seek you; my soul thirsts for you, my body longs for you, in a dry and weary land where there is no water."

According Philippians 3:8 (*Amplified version*) we are to count "everything as loss compared to the possession of the priceless privilege, the overwhelming preciousness, the surpassing worth and supreme advantage of knowing Christ Jesus our Lord".

The only intimacy that should matter to us is intimacy with our LORD. He should become our focus, our goal in life, our chief desire and the same shall flow to our spouses. True intimacy with God leaves us with a desire for deeper intimacy. The more we know our God, the more we want to know Him.

Like Paul went on to say in Phil. 3:10 (*Amplified version*)."For our determined purpose is that I may know him—that I may progressively become more deeply and intimately acquainted with Him, perceiving and recognizing and understanding the wonders of His Person more strongly and more clearly"

In *Enjoying Intimacy with God*. Admission to the inner circle of deepening intimacy with God is the outcome of deep desire. Only those who count such intimacy a prize worth sacrificing anything else for, are to attain it. If other intimacies are more desirable to us, we will not gain entry to that circle. A desire to know only the Lord and His character must be our motive for intimacy. If all I seek are His gifts or what He can do for me, I have a self-centered relationship based on God's "performance" in meeting my perceived needs. Instead, my desire to seek Him must be based on a longing just to know Him, to fellowship with Him, to enjoy His company. Same is true with marriage relationship. A desire to know only our spouse and their character must be our motive for intimacy with them. If all we seek are their gifts or what they can do for me, I have a self-centered relationship based on my spouse's "performance" in meeting my perceived needs. Instead, my desire to seek my spouse must be based on a longing just to know them, to fellowship with them, to enjoy their company.

Trust

To seek God in this way, I must be willing to admit that I am not the center of the universe, and that I am not self-sufficient. I cannot depend on anyone else but the Living God to fully and consistently care about what is best for me. To earnestly seek God, I must be willing to enter a relationship with Him on His terms by acknowledging my need and dependence upon Him.

In Psalm. 62:5-6 David wrote, "Find rest, O my soul, in God alone; my hope comes from him. He alone is my rock and my salvation"

In our life the greatest hindrance to developing intimacy with the Father is our bent to live our life in our own strength, to rely on our own insight, to think that we know what God wants us to do. We can easily distance ourselves from the Lord by trusting our feelings and our inclinations.

Similarly, the psalmist's feet came close to slipping when he observed the prosperity of the wicked and began to question God's justice. It wasn't until he came seeking the Lord that he was able to get an eternal perspective. Then he could confidently say,

In "Psalm 73:25-26. Whom have I in heaven but you? And earth has nothing I desire besides you. My flesh and my heart may fail, but God is the strength of my heart and my portion forever".

The psalmists knew that if they were left to their own devices, they would ultimately fail. They longed for God and God alone to be their rock and their salvation and so must we.

Abiding

I don't know about you, but for me desiring the fellowship of the Lord and fervently seeking His strength for my life motivates me to want to be with Him. When I found out that my wife is my intimate friend I truly desired to be intimate with her, then I planned to be with her as much as I can. David the psalmist wrote in

Psalm 27:4 (*TLB*) "The one thing I want from God, the thing I seek most of all, is the privilege of meditating in his Temple, living in his presence every day of my life, delighting in his incomparable perfections and glory"

Realistically, though, how can we live in His presence every day of our lives? God tells us in Psalm 91:1 "He who dwells in the shelter (secret place) of the Most High will rest in the shadow of the Almighty."

To dwell means to remain, abide, live, inhabit, exist. It conveys a constancy, a continuity, a daily communion with the Lord.

The relationship spoken of here is not an erratic, strange, bizarre, screwy or wacky visitation as need dictates. Jesus, in

John. 15:5 (*NASB*), taught, "I am the vine, you are the branches; he who abides in Me, and I in him, he bears much fruit; for apart from Me you can do nothing"

To bear the fruit of His character, which can only come from the intimacy of living with Him, we must choose to dwell in His shelter. It needs time to grow into Jesus the Vine do not expect to abide in Him unless you will give Him that time. We must come, my brethren, and day by day set ourselves by His feet, and meditate on this word of His power, with an eye fixed on Him alone. We must set ourselves in quiet trust before Him, waiting to hear His holy voice, the voice that is mightier than the storm that rends the rocks—breathing its quickening spirit within us, as He speaks: 'Abide in Me.'

Abiding is taking the time to nurture our friendship with the Lord. It is spending special time with Him daily, reading and studying His Word and conversing with Him. It is planning mornings or days alone with Him. Since He is our confidant, it is coming to Him first with our joys, hurts, and frustrations. Abiding is choosing to live in His presence and realizing that He is with us wherever we go. It is continually sharing our thoughts with Him throughout the day. It is meditating on His Scriptures so that I can know Him better. It is friendship sought on the deepest level. The decision to abide commits us to a lifelong process of developing intimacy with God and of "delighting in his incomparable perfections and glory."

Conformity

Important aspects of intimacy are desiring and acknowledging God's rightful place in our lives. We cannot presume upon His character,

GOD'S ORDER AND PURPOSE OF MARRIAGE

even with His great love and desire He has for us. Our God is a holy God. David in Psalm. 25:14 (*TLB*) wrote, "Friendship with God is reserved for those who reverence Him. God shares the secrets of His promise alone with those who reverence him"

What is essential to abiding in God is Reverence, and Respect, of Him. To reverence the Lord is to stand in awe of His majesty, His holiness, His power, His glory. To fear the Lord is to be concerned about ever displeasing Him. We must learn how to revere God in our relationship with Him and our spouses. Intimacy cannot occur "without respect."

In Ps. 15:1-2, A question is posed "who may dwell with God:" LORD, Who may dwell in God's sanctuary? Who may live on Your holy hill? He whose walk is blameless and who does what is righteous, who speaks the truth from his heart."

John 14:21 is one of the most concise verses on intimacy with God - "Whoever has my commands and obeys them, he is the one who loves me. He who loves me will be loved by my Father, and I too will love him and show myself to him."

To love God and want to grow in our knowledge of Him, we must obey His commands. It is in our obedience that God discloses Himself to us. Jesus said in

John 15:14 "You are my friends if you do what I command".

We can choose to pursue a lifestyle of purity by desiring and choosing to share in the secrets of His promise. The decision to be intimate with God will affect what books we read, what movies we watch, what music we listen to, what programs we watch on television who we hang out with and our relationship with our spouses. Abiding in His presence will alter our thought life, activities, and relationships. Our speech and actions will want to honor and reverence His Holy Name.

This does not mean that we will always be flawless. The essence of holiness is not that we are perfect, but that we never stop pursuing it." If we truly want to draw closer to God, then our heart's desire will be to please the Lord and to bring Him glory in all that we do.

A Settled Assurance

If intimacy with God is our ardent desire, then we will diligently seek Him for the friendship that only He can provide. We will trust Him with our lives and we will choose to honor Him by desiring to live righteously before Him.

If we are willing to know the Lord in this way, what will our lives be like? Shall we continually experience spiritual elatedness? Do we need to withdraw from the demands of daily life and just sit at the feet of Jesus?

Intimacy, for me, is essentially a settled assurance that God is *with* me and *for* me even though my feelings and circumstances may seem to deny His commitment to our relationship. It is trusting Him and His promise to never leave me or forsake me. It is knowing that He is with me in the reality of my life. It is not expecting some continual emotional assurance that He is my friend.

Day-to-day intimacy with God is putting on the Lord Jesus Christ" and entering the world confidently because the Lord is our Shield, our Defender, our intimate Friend. It is completely trusting God and His Word, not our feelings.

God does not have a secret society of intimate friends. We are as intimate with God as *we* choose to be. It is *our* craving, *our* abiding, *our* purity that will determine the depth of our intimacy with Him. Intimacy is understanding that I may feel "hinged" or "unhinged." It is knowing that I must sit at the feet of Jesus, so that I can walk with integrity as His friend. It is experiencing the closeness of the Lord and at other times wondering if He is near. Essentially, intimacy is abandonment of ourselves to the Lord—abandonment born out of trust and an intense longing to know the living God.

James said about Abraham, the father of the faithful.:

James 2:23 23 and the scripture was fulfilled which says, "Abraham believed God, and it was reckoned to him as righteousness"; and he was called the friend of God. (RSV)

Notice how James draws attention to the fact that Abraham was called *the friend of God*. The term "friend" is somewhat intimate and conveys a sense of closeness, trust, and sharing.

What is remarkable is that Abraham was termed *the friend of God*. The great, almighty, ever-present and all-powerful, all-knowing God was the one who made this statement. This was not Abraham's assessment of his relationship with God, nor how he thought about God. It was a statement that God made about Abraham.

James was quoting from - Isaiah 41:8 (RSV) But you, Israel, my servant, Jacob, whom I have chosen, the offspring of Abraham, my friend.

The children of Israel were God's servants and were the offspring of Abraham, who was God's friend. Just consider for a moment how remarkable these words are, and what a remarkable relationship they describe! Consider that a limited, physical, mortal being would be thought of by the all-powerful, Omnipotent God , all-knowing, Omniscient God, supreme God as His dearly beloved friend. Also consider that an imperfect man, made from the dust of the ground, would be viewed by the perfect Creator God composed of eternal spirit as one with whom He could have a warm, lasting and special friendship.

The words "*my friend*" are exactly how God did consider Abraham, and his relationship with God was a true and deep friendship.

One would raise some intriguing questions such as: How was such a relationship possible? What constitutes that kind of friendship? And can we enjoy that same kind of relationship with God, and if so how?

Part of the answer to this last question is "yes". God is not a respecter of persons. He too *calls us to* experience that same kind of friendship with God which Abraham enjoyed. But to do this we need to first examine what it is that makes friendships what they are to understand how we can, like Abraham, be called the friends of God.

Agreement is Necessary

We meet many people over the course of our lives , however, only a comparative few will ever become our close friends. One most obvious reasons are that of *agreement.* Our very best friends are those who agree with us on the greatest number of critical issues. *Friends think alike.* We can be on friendly terms with others, that is having pleasant and warm conversation with them, enjoy seeing them from time to time, but our closest friends are those who think like us. Clashing minds, diverging opinions and preferences do not really make for close relationships. In the words of the old saying, *birds of the same feathers flock together.* So, it was in the case of Abraham and his friendship with God. *He was in total agreement with God.*

Notice what God said about Abraham in Genesis 26. Here God is speaking to Isaac, and reconfirming the promises He gave to Abraham, now passed on to Isaac.

"Genesis 26:3-5 3 (RSV) Sojourn in this land, and I will be with you, and will bless you; for to you and to your descendants I will give all these lands, and I will fulfil the oath which I swore to Abraham your father. 4 I will multiply your descendants as the stars of heaven and will give to your descendants all these lands; and by your descendants all the nations of the earth shall bless themselves: 5 because Abraham obeyed my voice and kept my charge, my commandments, my statutes, and my laws."

Why did God make these unconditional promises to Abraham, and now pass them to Abraham's son Isaac? *Because Abraham obeyed God and kept His commandments* (v. 5). Abraham was in total agreement with God. He obeyed God precisely and, in every detail, even when he didn't know the outcome.

The prophet Amos posed the rhetorical question. "Amos 3:3(KJV) Can two walk together, except they be agreed?"

The word *agreed* is from the Hebrew *"ya`ad "* which means *to fix, appoint, assemble, meet, set, betr"oth, to meet, to meet by appointment.* The sense is not simply two walking in a common direction because they agree to it, but rather two agreeing to and making an appointment to come together and from there set out on a journey to a destination together. It is like saying to someone, *I'll meet you down at the Bank and we can go to the restaurant from there.* The Revise Standard Version captures this sense I "Amos 3:3 (RSV) "Do two walk together, unless they have made an appointment?" The context of the passage is given in the preceding verses. "Amos 3:1-2(RSV) ¹Hear this word that the LORD has spoken against you, O people of Israel, against the whole family which I brought up out of the land of Egypt: ²You only have I known of all the families of the earth; therefore, I will punish you for all your iniquities."

God made a covenant with Israel and promised to protect them and bless them. They in turn promised to obey Him and keep His laws. There was this coming together or agreement reached between Israel and God, about their plans to set out on the path to a new life in the Promised Land together. However, Israel let down their side of the agreement and veered off course. They repeatedly said, *we'll be a party to this, we agree to that,* but their word was not sure and so Israel and God were not able to walk together for any length of time. In this, Israel failed to follow the example of their forefather Abraham who went out of his homeland to a place God would show him, found out how God walked and came into agreement with it, walked in the paths of God's law, and did not follow the ways of this world.

Abraham was in precise and continuing agreement with God and that was one of the factors contributing to his friendship with God.

The parallel for us as Christian husband and wife is that we make an agreement with each other before God at marriage. We say, *Yes! We'll go where you want to go. We'll do what you want to do.* At wedding, we covenant with each other to love each other. We promise forgiveness, sticking together in good and inconvenient time. If we stick to our covenants with each other and make sure we submit ourselves to each other. If we let the Lord *set the pace* and *determine the route* we will take, then we will agree with Him and with each other which is one of the necessary factors for Him to call us His friends.

Loyalty and dependability

A second vital factor contributing to endearing friendships is that of *loyalty and dependability*. If you reflect on those people you count as your closest friends, it is those who have been loyal to you through thick and thin. It is those who you can count upon when the *chips are down*.

You don't ever want *"Fair-weather friend" in your relationships*. We use phrase *fair-weather friend* on those people who are pleased to be our friends when everything is fine and going smoothly. But, as soon as problems or troubles hit, they make themselves scarce. Fair-weather friends behave as they do because they look for what they can get out of a relationship rather than what they can give and put into it.

However, "True friends" are loyal and faithful to each other when the going is easy *and* when it gets tough. Loyal friends support each other. Faithful friends sacrifice for each other. Devoted friends are dependable. They're always there when needed.

On the eve of his death, Jesus Christ described the need for loyalty, dependability and sacrifice as a component of our friendship with him. Speaking to his disciples He said in John 15:13 Greater love has no man than this, that a man lay down his life for his friends. (RSV)

Our Lord Jesus was true to that statement. Christ showed us the ultimate expression of friendship in laying down his life for us as a sacrifice for our sins. He practiced what he preached. He went all the way for us.

Christ's sacrifice for us, as his articulation of devoted friendship toward us, should evoke loyalty and dependability from us as expressed in "John 15:14 (RSV) You are my friends if you do what I command you."

Christ was explaining that, just as he was prepared to go all the way for us, husbands need to go all the way for their wives in demonstrating our loyalty and reliability to them.

Of course, loyalty and dependability are only made fully manifest when we are tested and tempted to go against these principles. If your employer was to tell you that not working on the Sabbath will bring severe action against you, possibly even the loss of your job when you have a family to support and bills to pay the commandment to *remember the Sabbath to keep it holy* can become a severe test of loyalty to God and Christ.

But, when we are devoted friends of God and His Son, we *shall* be loyal to His commands, regardless of the consequences. God will see by our actions that He can depend upon us to *come through with the goods*. He will not let such loyalty go unrewarded. We will be recompensed in the process of time, either in this life or the age to come.

Abraham was a loyal friend of God in this way and the test God gave him of slaying Isaac demonstrated both his loyalty to God's commands and his dependability. When Abraham received the instructions to sacrifice Isaac, no doubt turmoil erupted in his mind. Human sacrifice was common in the false religions of the day. So, maybe, on one level the demand to sacrifice Isaac did not seem utterly unreasonable to Abraham. We don't have record of Abraham questioning God about it. On the other hand, Isaac was dearly loved by Abraham. He was the child of promise. It was through this son that God was going to fulfil the promises he had earlier made to Abraham in *"Genesis 17 When Abram was ninety-nine years old, the L*ORD *appeared to Abram and said to him, "I am Almighty God; walk before Me and be blameless. ² And I will make My covenant between Me and you and will multiply you exceedingly." ³ Then Abram fell on his face, and God talked with him, saying: ⁴ "As for Me, behold, My covenant is with you, and you shall be a father of many nations. ⁵ No longer shall your name be called Abram, but your name shall be Abraham; for I have made you a father of many nations. ⁶ I will make you exceedingly fruitful; and I will make nations of you, and kings shall come from you. ⁷ And I will establish My covenant between Me and you and your descendants after you in their generations, for an everlasting covenant, to be God to you and your descendants after you. ⁸ Also I give to you and your descendants after you the land in which you are a stranger, all the land of Canaan, as an everlasting possession; and I will be their God."*

⁹ And God said to Abraham: "As for you, you shall keep My covenant, you and your descendants after you throughout their generations. ¹⁰ This is My covenant which you shall keep, between Me and you and your descendants after you: Every male child among you shall be circumcised; ¹¹ and you shall be circumcised in the flesh of your foreskins, and it shall be a sign of the covenant between Me and you. ¹² He who is eight days old among you shall be circumcised, every male child in your generations, he who is born in your house or bought with money from any foreigner who is not your descendant. ¹³ He who is born in your house and he who is bought with your money must be circumcised, and My covenant shall be in your flesh for an everlasting covenant. ¹⁴ And the uncircumcised male child, who is not circumcised in the flesh of his foreskin, that person shall be cut off from his people; he has broken My covenant."

¹⁵ Then God said to Abraham, "As for Sarai your wife, you shall not call her name Sarai, but Sarah shall be her name. ¹⁶ And I will bless her and also give you a son by her; then I will bless her, and she shall be a mother of nations; kings of peoples shall be from her."

¹⁷ Then Abraham fell on his face and laughed, and said in his heart, "Shall a child be born to a man who is one hundred years old? And shall Sarah, who is ninety years old, bear a child?" ¹⁸ And Abraham said to God, "Oh, that Ishmael might live before You!"

¹⁹ Then God said: "No, Sarah your wife shall bear you a son, and you shall call his name Isaac; I will establish My covenant with him for an everlasting covenant, and with his descendants after him. ²⁰ And as for Ishmael, I have heard you. Behold, I have blessed him, and will make him fruitful, and will multiply him exceedingly. He shall beget twelve princes, and I will make him a great nation. ²¹ But My covenant I will establish with Isaac, whom Sarah shall bear to you at this set time next year." ²² Then He finished talking with him, and God went up from Abraham."

Abraham might also have reasoned that to slay another human being was murder and, therefore, sin. Regardless, Abraham did as God commanded and prepared to slay Isaac. He demonstrated his loyalty to his Creator. He demonstrated that he *could* be depended upon to carry out God's will no matter how difficult the assignment. Hence, God considered Abraham His friend.

The ability to confide

One more aspect of what constitutes devoted friendship is the ability of loyal friends *to confide in each other.*

This point builds upon the previous two points. Our closest friends are those in whom we can freely confide. They are those to whom we can communicate our deepest feelings and convictions, knowing we have a supportive listener and that we won't be betrayed.

With real friends we can discuss what is on our mind, we can share our joys, our observations, our plans, and even our sorrows and regrets. When there is deep and intense friendship, nothing needs to be held back.

Christ described this dimension of friendship in *"John 15:15(RSV) No longer do I call you servants, for the servant does not know what his master is doing; but I have called you friends, for all that I have heard from my Father I have made known to you."*

Friends confide in each other, and Christ considers us to be such good friends of his that he can confide in us and share all the plans, hopes and dreams he and the Father have for us and mankind. He says that *all* that he has heard of the Father, he has made known to us.

Now, depending on the degree of our friendship with others, we tend to hold back certain information. There are very few people we share everything with. Only our closest friends get that kind of treatment. But Christ is demonstrating here that he considers us his closest and most sympathetic friends.

God through Christ set a precedent by extending friendship to us through His willingness to confide in us so we can follow His example with spouses. Therefore, we are to return that friendship to Him by confiding in Him and our spouses. We are to spend time talking to Him, pouring out our hearts to Him, and telling Him of our every need and desire.

Abraham was a man of that caliber, so much so that God truly regarded him as a close confidant.

In *Genesis 18:17-19(RSV)* [17] *The LORD said, "Shall I hide from Abraham what I am about to do,* [18] *seeing that Abraham shall become a great and mighty nation, and all the nations of the earth shall bless themselves by him?* [19]*No, for I have chosen him, that he may charge his children and his household after him to keep the way of the LORD by doing righteousness and justice; so that the LORD may bring to Abraham what he has promised him. Compare Genesis 18:19(KJV)*

GOD'S ORDER AND PURPOSE OF MARRIAGE

For I know him, that he will command his children and his household after him,"

Abraham enjoyed this marvelous closeness with God through Christ who acted as God's messenger. Christ and two angels had just met with Abraham to tell him how Sarah would bear Isaac, as a fulfilment of God's promise to him. The angels then continued their journey to Sodom to save Lot and his family from being destroyed in the overthrow of that city.

God *knew* what Abraham was like as a person and felt assured in confiding in him. By the same token, Abraham was open with God and spoke freely with Him the way God expect of spouses and as he did with Christ in the exchange that covers the next few verses.

Genesis 18:20-33(RSV) 20 Then the LORD said, "Because the outcry against Sodom and Gomorrah is great and their sin is very grave, 21 I will go down to see whether they have done altogether according to the outcry which has come to me; and if not, I will know." 22 So the men turned from there, and went toward Sodom; but Abraham still stood before the LORD. 23 Then Abraham drew near, and said, "Wilt thou indeed destroy the righteous with the wicked? 24 Suppose there are fifty righteous within the city; wilt thou then destroy the place and not spare it for the fifty righteous who are in it? 25 Far be it from thee to do such a thing, to slay the righteous with the wicked, so that the righteous fare as the wicked! Far be that from thee! Shall not the Judge of all the earth do right?" 26 And the LORD said, "If I find at Sodom fifty righteous in the city, I will spare the whole place for their sake." 27 Abraham answered, "Behold, I have taken upon myself to speak to the Lord, I who am but dust and ashes. 28 Suppose five of the fifty righteous are lacking? Wilt thou destroy the whole city for lack of five?" And he said, "I will not destroy it if I find forty-five there." 29 Again he spoke to him, and said, "Suppose forty are found there." He answered, "For the sake of forty I will not do it." 30 Then he said, "Oh let not the Lord be angry, and I will speak. Suppose thirty are found there." He answered, "I will not do it, if I find thirty there." 31 He said, "Behold, I have taken upon myself to speak to the Lord. Suppose twenty are found there." He answered, "For the sake of twenty I will not destroy it." ³²*Then he said, "Oh let not the Lord be angry, and I will speak again but this once. Suppose ten are found there." He answered, "For the sake of ten I will not destroy it."* ³³*And the LORD went his way, when he had finished speaking to Abraham; and Abraham returned to his place.*

The relationship Abraham enjoyed with God was a remarkable one by human standards – but tremendously encouraging for us. God is not partial. He is not a respecter of persons. God doesn't involve Himself in cliques or narrow, exclusive groups of people that only a few can enter. Rather, He extends the hand of friendship to all of those in His family. If we follow the example of our spiritual forefather Abraham by *agreeing with* God, displaying *loyalty and dependability* towards God, *and freely confiding* in Him in all matters, then we too will be called the friends of God. As children of God with His Image, Likeness, similitude, and resemblance (character, nature and authority) we must similarly relate with our wives.

You might be surprised to know that the Bible provides examples and specific principles to help us understand exactly how to be a friend of God. There and then is when you can become friend to your wife.

Chapter 14

Friends with God and Wife

First a friend of God is one who values His presence above all else. Moses had spent the last forty days alone with God. While there he had received both the law and the rules of worship from God. His dismay was overwhelming when upon his return to the camp found the people engaged in idolatrous worship and licentious goatish, hypersexual behavior! In fact, were it not for the intercession of Moses, God would have destroyed His people right there in the wilderness.

Consequentially it turned out that the Lord refused to lead them any further by His presence. From now on He would merely use an angel to direct their journey.

But Moses refused to accept such a proposition. If the Lord did not travel with them, Moses was staying put! *"Exodus 33:15 Then he said to Him, "If Your Presence does not go with us, do not bring us up from here."* The conversation Moses shared with the Lord revealed Moses' supreme desire to know God intimately. Read with me "Exodus 33:11 And the LORD spoke unto Moses face to face, as a man ***speaks unto his friend***. And he turned again into the camp, but his servant Joshua, the son of Nun, a young man, departed not out of the tabernacle." Moses wanted the presence of Almighty God more than he wanted the Promised Land with all its prospects of stability and fruitfulness.

Friends of God are they who prioritize their relationship with Him, not allowing the work of God ever to replace the God of the work in their devotion. In the same manner husband, you must prioritize your relationship and friendship to your wife. The Father prioritized His friendship with the Son and Christ with the church. Your friendship with God your friendship with your wife.

Second a friend of God will live a life of faith. The foundation of every healthy relationship is trust. The greatest expression of my friendship with my wife is that I trust her no matter what. Abraham is best noted for his faith in God; in fact, he has been called, "The Father of Faith." James 2:23And the scripture was fulfilled which saith, Abraham believed God, and it was imputed unto him for righteousness: and he was called *the Friend of God*

Always remember that it is faith that pleases God. "Hebrews 11:6 But without faith *it is* impossible to please *Him,* for he who comes to God must believe that He is, and *that* He is a rewarder of those who diligently seek Him." Abraham believed that God would make of him a great nation even when his wife was barren and beyond childbearing years. All he had to let go on was the explicit Word of God. Circumstances, biology, and human reasoning shouted their objections to Abraham's faith.

What is it you have refused to put into practice that God clearly said to you in His Word? Perhaps it is tithing, soulwinning, strife, or unforgiveness, untamed tongue etc.! Who are those shouting their objections to your faith? Friends of God take Him at His Word. They know that God would never ask them to do something that was not mutually beneficial. Abraham believed God and was given the timeless label, "Friend of God" Read with me in "2 Chronicles 20:7 *Are* You not our God, *who* drove out the inhabitants of this land before Your people Israel, and gave it to the descendants of Abraham Your friend forever?" And "Isaiah 41:8 "But you, Israel, *are* My servant, Jacob whom I have chosen, The descendants of Abraham My friend."

Is that desire true of you for your wife? Your friendship with God your friendship with your wife.

Third a friend of God is one who joyfully seeks His benefit and advances His agenda. We are taught a great lesson in the dwindling moments of John the Baptist public ministry. His own disciples complained that the new ministry of Jesus Christ had eclipsed their own both in popularity and in the sheer number of those baptized. To adjust their carnal thinking, John employed the illustration of a friend as best man. Please read with me in **"John 3:29 He that has the bride is the bridegroom, but the *friend of the bridegroom*, which stands and hears him, rejoices greatly because of the bridegroom's voice: this my joy therefore is fulfilled."**

Your loyal friend would rather have you bask in the limelight, that you receive the compliment, and that you enjoy the credit. The closer one's relationship with God, the less he will be concerned about personal recognition. It is enough for God's friends and supremely satisfying to them that God receives the glory! Examine your own heart and whether that desire is true of you for your wife? Your friendship with God your friendship with your wife.

Fourth a friend of God will carefully guard his affections and amusements. Friendship with God cannot co-exist simultaneously with the friendship of the world. Please read what the bible records in the books of James and 1st John. "James 4:4 Ye adulterers and adulteresses, know ye not that the friendship of the world is enmity with God? whosoever therefore will be a friend of the world is the enemy of God." "1 John 2:15-17 [15] Do not love the world or the things in the world. If anyone loves the world, the love of the Father is not in him. [16] For all that *is* in the world—the lust of the flesh, the lust of the eyes, and the pride of life—is not of the Father but is of the world. [17] And the world is passing away, and the lust of it; but he who does the will of God abides forever." Wickedness and worship cannot coexist. Friends of God are those whose love for God transcends the allure of the world system with its coexisting lusts and pride. Reviewing your schedule and your priorities will certainly tell you whether you are a friend of the world or a friend of God. They will tell you the truth about your friendships. Is friendship with God and your wife a priority? **Your friendship with God your friendship with your wife.**

Fifth a friend of God is privy to exclusive information and is supremely reliable with it. Think for a moment about your closest friends. They are the ones with whom you can share even the most confidential information. You trust them and know that they will always act in your best interest. In humanly terms, the best friends of Jesus were His disciples. With them He shared His deepest thoughts, emotions, and visions. To them He carefully provided instruction and expectation. Is this the case with your wife? Your friendship with God your friendship with your wife.

"John 15:13-15 - Greater love hath no man than this, that a man lay down his life for his *friends. Ye are my friends*, if ye do whatsoever I command you. Henceforth I call you not servants; for the servant knows not what his lord doeth: but *I have called you friends*; for all things that I have heard of my Father I have made known unto you."

A loyal friend of Christ is faithful to the exclusive information received from Him (His Word), and one must be true to keep his commitments to it. The request of a friend is a royal command. This statement is never truer than when it applies to the life of the follower of Jesus Christ! When it comes right down to it, most of us would have to admit that we are more acquaintances of God than we are His friends. May God help us to consider these principles, apply their truth, and enjoy their marvelous benefits.

Chapter 15

Make friends with your wife

First she is sent from God in heaven to you. She is from on high and she is of a high class. Please don't lower her to an inferior class. The scripture in Proverbs 19:14 tells you that a prudent wife is from the Lord. "***Houses and riches are an inheritance from fathers, but a prudent wife is from the Lord.***" In Proverbs 18:22 & 24 referring to your wife as your friend says "v22 ***He who finds a wife finds good thing and obtains favor from the Lord. V24 A man who has friends must himself be friendly.***" Referring to the wife the verse continues with the same thought to say, "***But there is a friend who sticks closer than a brother,***" **Your wife.** She is your best friend who sticks closer than a brother. All others are acquaintances and will leave you for the dead for any reason. Your wife will be the last one to leave you. She will be there to support and help you through life's challenges. She has the grace to cling on you. Being your wife's friend helps you bear her grieves and burdens. Friendship plays a strategic role to your wife's emotional growth and mental health. It boosts her happiness. speaking to your wife as a friend lowers her blood pressure reducing the risk of depression. Hugging, listening, sharing, connecting, and celebrating life with friends decreases stress. That is what a friend, your wife is there for, she helps you live longer. That is the power of friendship.

Second she is God's daughter and He demands you her truly and sincerely. It is obvious that words communicate love, but much so do actions of intersession where you are not looking to benefit yourself and sacrificial actions where you give up something to benefit her. Husbands you must endeavor to do both. This is what the Apostle John meant in *1 John 3:18) - "let us not love with words or tongue, but with actions and in truth"*. The missing ingredients in male leadership in homes include sacrificial and intersession actions. When was the last time you gave up something for your wife—something you genuinely valued, like foregoing buying a suit and have your wife buy thirty outfits one for each day of the month. Taking public transportation to work and your wife drives the family car to work or to take care of errands. Sometimes you need to give up something you enjoy so your wife can have a break and see your love for her. Husband you are to intercede for your wife not only in words but in actions where you do everything for her benefit. Loving husbands build up their wives. They motivate, inspire, and pull them up and together each achieves more.

Third she will become God's bride when you depart, abandon, and relinquish your leadership responsibilities. Husbands devoid of love for their wives are unsuccessful. They shamefully hate, blame, complain, and are bitter with their wives who desperately long for their love and kindness. Wives married to these hateful, blaming, complaining, bitter, egocentric, self-centered husbands are literally widows in the spiritual sense of widowhood. These husbands' love conscience is dead. Therefore, they do not have any love to give you. Instead they abuse you verbally, mentally, emotionally, and physically. He stopped being your husband by the virtue of his unbecoming behavior to you and Jehovah took over as your husband. One can only give what they have. Don't look for love from him. The LORD has called you for being forsaken and grieved in your spirit when you were refused, rejected and left for the dead. Look to God for your love. He loves you with an everlasting love. He has become your husband.

Isaiah 54:2-8 "² Enlarge the place of your tent and let them stretch out the curtains of your dwellings; Do not spare. Lengthen your cords, and strengthen your stakes ³………. ⁴…..Do not fear, for you will not be ashamed; Neither be disgraced, for you will not be put to shame; For you will forget the shame of your youth, and will not remember the reproach of your widowhood anymore. ⁵For your Maker is your husband, The LORD of hosts is His Name And your Redeemer is the Lord God of your faith; He is called the God of the whole earth. ⁶ For the LORD has called you Like a woman forsaken and grieved in spirit, like a youthful wife when you were refused," Says your God. ⁷ "………But with great mercies I will gather you. ⁸………. But with everlasting kindness I will have mercy on you," Says the LORD, your Redeemer."

God sees the suffering of His daughters in the hands of hateful husbands with unrenewed minds, wills that are not bound to the will of God, emotions that are not controlled by Holy Spirit, and attitudes that are not expressions of the fruit of the Holy Spirit. He sees the oppression and hears the cry of His daughters and comes for their deliverance. Please read what the scripture reads in **Ezekiel 16:6-14**. *⁶ "And when I passed by you and saw you struggling in your own blood, I said to you in your blood, 'Live!' Yes, I said to you in your blood, 'Live!' ⁷ I made you thrive like a plant in the field; and you grew, matured, and became very beautiful. Your breasts were formed, your hair grew, but you were naked and bare. ⁸"When I passed by you again and looked upon you, indeed your time was the time of love; so, I spread My wing over you and covered your nakedness. Yes, I swore an oath to you and entered a covenant with you, and you became Mine," says the Lord GOD. ⁹"Then I washed you in water; yes, I thoroughly washed off your blood, and I anointed you with oil. ¹⁰ I clothed you in embroidered cloth and gave you sandals of badger skin; I clothed you with fine linen and covered you with silk. ¹¹ I adorned you with ornaments, put bracelets on your wrists, and a chain on your neck. ¹² And I put a jewel in your nose, earrings in your ears, and a beautiful crown on your head. ¹³ Thus you were adorned with gold and silver, and your clothing was of fine linen, silk, and embroidered cloth. You ate pastry of fine flour, honey, and oil. You were exceedingly beautiful* *and succeeded to royalty. ¹⁴ Your fame went out among the nations because of your beauty, for it was perfect through My splendor which I had bestowed on you," says the Lord GOD.*

Fourth **Serve your wife.** Being head of your wife does not mean being her master, but her servant. Christ is our model for this type of leadership. Leadership is not something you learn; it's something you discover. Jesus did not just talk about serving; He demonstrated it when he washed His disciples' feet.

"John 13:1-17 ¹³Now before the Feast of the Passover, when Jesus knew that His hour had come that He should depart from this world to the Father, having loved His own who were in the world, He loved them to the end. ² And supper being ended,[a] the devil having already put it into the heart of Judas Iscariot, Simon's son, to betray Him, ³ Jesus, knowing that the Father had given all things into His hands, and that He had come from God and was going to God, ⁴ rose from supper and laid aside His garments, took a towel and girded Himself. ⁵ After that, He poured water into a basin and began to wash the disciples' feet, and to wipe them with the towel with which He was girded. ⁶ Then He came to Simon Peter. And Peter said to Him, "Lord, are You washing my feet?" ⁷ Jesus answered and said to him, "What I am doing you do not understand now, but you will know after this." ⁸ Peter said to Him, "You shall never wash my feet!" Jesus answered him, "If I do not wash you, you have no part with Me." ⁹ Simon Peter said to Him, "Lord, not my feet only, but also my hands and my head!" ¹⁰ Jesus said to him, "He who is bathed needs only to wash his feet, but is completely clean; and you are clean, but not all of you." ¹¹ For He knew who would betray Him; therefore He said, "You are not all clean."

¹² So when He had washed their feet, taken His garments, and sat down again, He said to them, "Do you know what I have done to you? ¹³ You call Me Teacher and Lord, and you say well, for so I am. ¹⁴ If I then, your Lord and Teacher, have washed your feet, you also ought to wash one another's feet. ¹⁵ For I have given you an example, that you should do as I have done to you. ¹⁶ Most assuredly, I say to you, a servant is not greater than his master; nor is he who is sent greater than he who sent him. ¹⁷ If you know these things, blessed are you if you do them".

Christ, the Head of the Church, took on the very nature of a servant. when He was made in human likeness **"Philippians 2:7 (NKJV)** *⁷ but made Himself of no reputation, taking the form of a bondservant, and coming in the likeness of men."*

One of the best ways to serve your wife is to understand her needs and try to meet them. Do you know what your wife's top three needs are right now? If she is a young mother, she has a certain set of basic needs. If your children are grown and gone and you are in the empty nest, your wife has a distinct set of needs that you are to meet. What is she worried about? What troubles her? What type of pressure does she feel? Learn the answers to questions like thses and then do what you are supposed to do to reduce her worries, her troubles, her pressures.

What do you know about your wife's hopes and dreams? I bet she has plenty—do you know what they are? Are you cultivating her gifts? If she has a knack for decorating, do you help her develop that?

Another way of serving your wife is by *providing for her*. This provision first involves assuming responsibility for meeting the material needs of the family. ***1 Timothy 5:8 tells us, "But if anyone does not provide for his own, and especially for those of his household, he has denied the faith, and is worse than an unbeliever."***

Providing for your wife also means taking the initiative in helping meet her spiritual needs. You do this by modeling godly character, by praying with her, by spending time together in God's Word, by planning and discussing your future together, and by looking for ways to encourage her spiritually underscores the significance of husbands' treatment to their wives like Christ does to His bride, the church.

*Ephesians 5:25-27 – "**²⁵ Husbands, love your wives, just as Christ also loved the church and gave Himself for her, ²⁶ that He might sanctify and cleanse her with the washing of water by the word, ²⁷ that He might present her to Himself a glorious church, not having spot or wrinkle or any such thing, but that she should be holy and without blemish."*

To be a leader, a lover, and a servant is to accommodate your life to the life of the gift God has given you, **your wife.** Give up your life for her and, at the judgment seat of Christ, He will say, "Well done, thou good and faithful servant."

Chapter 16

My wife, my Wealth

In Proverbs in 19:13 Expanded Bible version reads this way: "Houses and wealth are inherited from parents, but a wise, insightful wife is a gift from the LORD." And Contemporary English Version reads: "You may inherit all you own from your parents, but a sensible wife is a gift from the LORD."

A gift is a special ability, notable capacity, talent or endowment. The In Proverbs 18:16 A man's(male and female) gift makes room for him (male and female) and brings him(male and female) before great men(males and females).

A wife is a gift from the Lord and makes room or opportunities for the husband to cease.

A godly wife is a gift, a special ability, notable capacity, talent and endowment to influence her husband for the better. *She has a high level of godliness. She has her base in God and who He is first and foremost. Her godliness is about God not herself. She hurts when her husband or children stray because they are estranged from God, more than how it reflects her.* A wife this caliber spends time and intentionally seek after God.

A godly wife, a gift, a special ability, notable capacity, talent and endowment **actively seeks wisdom from Scripture.** *She is full of* *wisdom. She trains her mind to think as the Bible thinks.* A godly wife, a gift, a special ability, notable capacity, talent and endowment is *so steeped in Scripture that what Scripture teaches is just her natural disposition. That is what comes out of her because she has trained her mind to think as God thinks, through the study of Scripture.*

A godly wife, a gift, a special ability, notable capacity, talent and endowment is m**arked by faith, peace and love.** *Her core value is in who God is, is in her faith. She is marked by Peace because she knows God is her peace that means nothing is missing, nothing is lacking, and nothing is broken. She is marked by love because love is her disposition toward others. She is willing to love. She is both the lioness and confronts out of love, and she is the soft nurturing mom who comforts and encourages.*

A godly wife, a gift, a special ability, notable capacity, talent and endowment **is** ultimately wife of power, joy, and purpose. She *has the Holy Spirit within her. She has learned to surrender her rights to the Holy Spirit. Your godly wife*, a gift from God, a special ability, notable capacity, talent and endowment *knows it is not about her natural gifts nor is it about what she is able to do. She offers herself to God and He works in her in ways she couldn't even imagine both to will and to do His good pleasure.*

There is no joy that rivals a woman who believes she is doing what God has created her to do, with God's power working within her. Sense of purpose and happiness creates joy in a creates in a godly wife, a gift, a special ability, notable capacity, talent and endowment. When a godly wife, a gift from God walks with humility and has God as her rock and foundation she influences and impacts her husband's heart. Here is the kicker wives, husbands are influenced by people they respect not necessarily by people they love.

Many a husband are living beneath their privileges for mistreating their wives. Treating your wife well has some very Tangible Benefits. Wives are like nature; they multiply what you give them and give it back to you. Learn right early in life to treat your wife right. Give your wife love, she will adore you, give her respect and honor, she will worship you, give her time, she will give you a life time, give her money, she will give you an investment.

On the contrary, if you give your wife slaps, life will slap you back. You oppress your wife, society will oppress you.

Leviticus 24:19-21(NKJV) [19] ***'If a man causes disfigurement of his neighbor, as he has done, so shall it be done to him—*** [20] ***fracture for fracture, eye for eye, tooth for tooth; as he has caused disfigurement of a man, so shall it be done to him.*** [21] ***And whoever kills an animal shall restore it; but whoever kills a man shall be put to death.***

Examples would be societies and communities that mistreat their women. They give their women slaps and life slaps them back. They oppress their women and society oppresses them. There is a major world religion that oppresses its women. Consequentially they are at war with basically everyone everywhere across the globe.

Any husband that treats his wife like trash ends up as trash. Observe anyone who treats his wife like a queen they end up as kings. All you husbands will have to try it, after having lived on your ways for decades, just try this Principle and you will be amazed to see your prosperity too. Believe in ***"My Wife, My Wealth"*** and God will bless you abundantly.

Chapter 17

A Husband's Treatment to His Wife

Wife is the greatest gift God has given to male man. There is nothing more precious than a husband and wife who have lived their whole lives in a covenant of love and marriage.

Husband and wife who love God and love each other are to live together "till death do they part." When husband and wife pursue their marriage on God's terms, they find that their marriage is happy and fulfilling.

According to Ephesians 5:22-33: Husband you are the head of your wife even as Christ is the head of the church, his body, **you are her Savior.** By loving your wife, you love yourself. For no one ever hated his own flesh, but nourishes and cherishes it, just as Christ does the church, because we are members of his body.

Husbands you are to love your wives without conditions as your own bodies. Your wives are made to be loved to function effectively. You are to give yourselves up for your wives. Husbands you are to sanctify your wives. You are to have your wives cleansed by the washing of water with the word. Husband you are to present your wife to yourself in splendor, without spot or wrinkle or any such thing, that she might be holy and without blemish. You are to love your wife as yourself. Any male man treating his wife unkindly is acting very ignorantly. You are not only disobeying God, but you are deceiving yourself.

Only an ignorant husband could think that abusing his wife will be a benefit to him. Husbands wise up, the better you treat your wives, the more your wives will respond with honor and respect to you. When you fail to love your wife, she will respond with disrespect. When husbands sense disrespect from their wives, they often act in ways that are unbecoming. Experiences of being disrespected and unloved ruin marriage. When husbands show love and wives respect, their marriages prosper and develop. Husband, you can make your marriage heaven on earth, if you can learn to demonstrate Christ like love to your wife. If a disrespected husband was to love his wife anyway, he would start restoring that marriage. A wise husband pays attention to his wife. He sees the things that she needs to find happiness in this life. A wife needs to feel that her husband is close to her and cares about her. A husband who keeps distance from his wife, he makes her feel unloved. A wife needs a husband who will open up enough to share his thoughts and feelings with her. She will feel unwanted or unneeded when he closes and shuts her out of his life.

When he keeps his life secret from her, she feels he doesn't love her enough to trust her. A wife needs to know her husband is loyal to the marriage, that he is not looking elsewhere. A wife also needs to know the husband sees her as the most important person in his life beside God. A wife needs to know that her husband cherishes, loves and honors her. The most terrific thing a husband can do is to love his wife.

1 Corinthians 13:4-8 says, "Love is patient and kind; love does not envy or boast; it is not arrogant or rude. It does not insist on its own way; it is not irritable or resentful; it does not rejoice at wrong doing but rejoices with the truth. Love bears all things, believes all things, hopes all things, endures all things. Love never ends."

Husbands must learn how to love their wives. Love demands that we set "self" aside. You cannot love your wife if selfishness and self-centeredness is your way. Love rules out envy, arrogance and rudeness.

Love learns to cover a multitude of wrongs and is not irritated all the time. Love puts up with a lot of wifey demands, believes and hopes the best for your wife. Love is enduring. Love for your wife is the determination to put her best interests before your own, regardless of the cost.

Jesus loved the church like that, and He asks husbands to love their wives that way. Loving your wife involves taking the time to be close to her and to listen to her. The happiest spouses spend quality time with each other creating and bringing forth, speaking and listening to each other. Happily married spouses spend quality time each day in constructive conversation. Turn the television off, get away from the computer and other distractors and talk face to face with each other.

A wise husband will take the time share his life with the wife he loves. He wants to know about her and is willing to invest his life in her by listening. Failing to pay attention to your wife is to say to her that you do not care about what she must say to you. Such behavior is abusive not loving.

James 1:19-20, says ***"Know this, my beloved brothers: let every person be quick to hear, slow to speak, slow to anger; for the anger of man does not produce the righteousness that God requires."***

Much of the anger in our homes would go away if husbands would take the time to listen and understand the wives they love. Listen to your wife, let her finish her sentences, don't act rashly or hastily. Try to understand her life from her point of view. Treat your wife kindly. 1 Peter 3:7 says: "Likewise, husbands, live with your wives in an understanding way, showing honor to the wife as the weaker vessel, since they are heirs with you of the grace of life, so that your prayers may not be hindered."

Some husbands have a bad attitude that because they are the head of the wife, that this position of authority gives them the right to dominate or abuse their wives with their power.

GOD'S ORDER AND PURPOSE OF MARRIAGE

Any man who treats his wife like a doormat is violating the will of God. Abusive power is a marriage killer. Husbands, treat your wife kindly, tell your wife how important and valuable she is to you. Watch for the loving smile on her face when you do! Proverbs 31:10-11 says, "An excellent wife, who can find? For her worth is far above jewels. The heart of her husband trusts in her, and he will have no lack of gain." Notice how the wise husband trusts his wife's judgments and realizes how empowered to prosper he is to have her. It is utter foolishness for a man to expect his wife to submit to him and meet all his needs, while he treats her unkindly. Husbands, love your wives. Jesus taught in the Sermon on the Mount, "In everything, therefore, treat people the same way you want them to treat you, for this is the Law and the Prophets" (Matthew 7:12). I am amazed at times how kind and good people can be to those outside the family but treat their own families with disrespect. Husbands and wives both should obey the golden rule with their spouses. If we could see ourselves as we really are and how we treat our families, we might be quite shocked. If we had a tape recording of our words or a video of our actions, we might see ourselves the way our families see us. Some folks never consider how difficult they make their family's lives. That's why, every now and then, it is good for all of us to step back and take a long look at how we have treated our families. Empathy is the ability to see things through the eyes of another and to feel what he or she is feeling. Sometimes we look at ourselves through other's eyes. When we do that, what shall we see? Shall we like what we see? Jesus also cautions husbands in the Sermon on the Mount to control their eyes and their thoughts about women other than their wives. He said in Matthew 5:27-30: *"You have heard that it was said, 'YOU SHALL NOT COMMIT ADULTERY'; but I say to you that everyone who looks at a woman (not his wife) with lust for her has already committed adultery with her in his heart. If your right eye makes you stumble, tear it out and throw it from you; for it is better for you to lose one of the parts of your body, than for your whole body to be thrown into hell. If your right hand makes you stumble, cut it off and throw it from you; for it is better for you to lose one of the parts of your body, than for your whole body to go into hell."*

Looking at other women is for many men a terrible habit. It says to his wife that she is not the focus of his attention, that there is someone better out there. Job knew that a righteous man kept his eyes in control. He said in Job 31:1-4, *"I have made a covenant with my eyes; how then could I gaze at a virgin? What would be my portion from God above and my heritage from the Almighty on high? Is not calamity for the unrighteous, and disaster for the workers of iniquity? Does not he see my ways and number all my steps?"* Unfortunately, many husbands are caught up in the habit of pornography. Looking at smutty pictures and videos, they commit adultery in their hearts by turning their attention to someone other than their wife. Husbands are not alone in this sinful behavior; many wives are now habitual viewers of pornography. When pornography fills the heart, it won't be long before adultery of the heart becomes adultery in life. More than a few homes today are being destroyed by pornography in videos, in literature, and on the internet. Pornography is adultery, fornication and prostitution. Wise husbands who love God and their wives keep their hearts, eyes, and their lives clean. A wise husband will also be a spiritual leader in his home. One of the most spiritually important things couples can do is spend time together believing, singing, praying, and reading the Bible. There is excellent value in a husband and wife privately believing together every day. Believing together allows husbands and wives to take their burdens together to God the Father. It allows them to express in each other's presence and in the presence of God their concerns and needs. When two people pray with each other, they develop a spiritual intimacy and unity that builds their relationship. Christian marriages, where God is the center of the home, where love is the order of the day, and where patience and forgiveness are present, and where God's laws are obeyed, almost never end in divorce. God's ways are not only right ways; they are the best ways. When people truly live the Christian life, the way God intended, they find their marriages to be the happiest and most loving. Husbands, do your best to make your home what God would have it to be. Have private devotions at home but also go to church and get involved in the work of the Lord. God's way is truly, truly, a way of blessing. Not every Christian man or woman is happily married. What can you do if your needs are currently not being met? First, identify and acknowledge your hurts to yourself and your spouse. Hurts cannot be healed, and needs cannot be met, if they are ignored. Most men have a tough time reading their wives minds; wives need to spell it out for their husbands. Each one needs to talk openly, honestly, and lovingly to the other about what he or she needs. Now, the emotional baggage caused by unmet needs doesn't just "go away" with time. Husbands and wives both need to acknowledge their feelings of anger, bitterness or resentment to their spouses. But once you have taken the time to reveal a fault, then forgive your spouse. Paul said in Ephesians 4:31-32, *"Let all bitterness and wrath and anger and clamor and slander be put away from you, along with all malice. Be kind to one another, tenderhearted, forgiving one another, as God in Christ forgave you."* The most important thing any couple can do is learn how to settle their differences. Everyone needs to learn the fine art of apologizing and forgiving. All couples have disagreements, but the ones who survive and thrive learn how to put problems behind them. They learn how to talk out a problem and solve it in line the word of God rather than let it fester and destroy the marriage. Peter said, "Love covers a multitude of sins" (1 Peter 4:8). God is so wonderful to forgive us; His forgiveness teaches us how to forgive even the deepest of hurts. God loved you and me enough to send Jesus to die for our sins and to cleanse us from all unrighteousness. When we place our faith in Christ as Lord and the Son of God, when we turn away from sin in repentance, when we confess the name of Jesus before others, and after we are baptized, the Lord forgives us. **(Acts 2:38 Then Peter said to them, "Repent, and let every one of you be baptized in the name of Jesus Christ for the remission of sins; and you shall receive the gift of the Holy Spirit.).** After you are born again in your spirit, you must now work out your soul salvation with fear and trembling.

Philippians 2:12-13 (NKJV) [12] Therefore, my beloved, as you have always obeyed, not as in my presence only, but now much more in my absence, work out your own salvation with fear and trembling; [13] for it is God who works in you both to will and to do for His good pleasure.

The goodness of God towards us makes us want to be good too. If the Lord could forgive all our sins, we can forgive others. I hope and pray that you won't let anything come between you and God. Why not today get your life right with God? Some need to obey the gospel, and some need to be restored to a right relationship with the Father. Don't wait another day. Get right with God today.

God is so wonderful to forgive us; His forgiveness teaches us how to forgive even the deepest of hurts. God loved you and me enough to send Jesus to die for our sins and to cleanse us from all unrighteousness. When we place our faith in Christ as Lord and the Son of God, when we turn away from sin in repentance, when we confess the name of Jesus before others, and after we are baptized, the Lord forgives us (Acts 2:38). The goodness of God towards us makes us want to be good too. If the Lord could forgive all our sins, we can forgive others. I hope and pray that you won't let anything come between you and God. Why not today get your life right with God. Some need to obey the gospel, and some need to be restored to a right relationship with the Father. Don't wait another day. Get right with God today.

Marriage is a God's Idea

Where there is anything that is designed there is a designer. There is always a mastermind behind the masterpiece, whether a vehicle, building, train or even marriage. God, the mastermind of marriage, also has a plan for how marriage works best.

Understanding God's design and plan for marital love can be overwhelming because there are contradicting and varying messages everywhere. A lot of these messages are found in books, magazines, movies and music. Consequently, many couples fall into the trap of looking everywhere but to the Designer to find out what God intended for marriage. If you have tried understanding marriage through the world, there's a better way.

GOD'S ORDER AND PURPOSE OF MARRIAGE

The Holy Spirit who is the teacher and reminder of all things. He will teach you how you can draw from the design that God has for marriage in His word. The scripture will show you how marriage is created out of divine order, based on a covenant relationship, reflects our relationship with God and truly has a greater impact in our lives than many have assumed. Actualizations of God's way of doing things will help you to experience a greater sense of fulfillment and a lifelong perspective for your marriage relationship.

Chapter 18

Praising Your Wife

In the Bible in the book of Song of Solomon, we read of an example of the way human life finds its highest fulfillment in the love of man and woman. In the same way the spiritual life finds its highest fulfillment in the love of God for His people and Christ for His church. The book reads like scenes in a drama, play, or movie with three main speakers; The bride (Shulamite) Her beloved (the king, Solomon) and a chorus (daughters of Jerusalem). Love is the key word in the song. This love which presents the passionate desire between a man and a woman celebrates the joyous potential of marriage in light of sworn covenant principles. The basis of all human love should be covenant love, the master metaphor of the bible. The covenant love also is the basis of relationship between God and man. Therefore, the song applies properly to both marriage and to the covenant history. The Shulamite therefore personifies the wife in an ideal marriage and the covenant people and their history in the promised land under the blessings of Solomonic love.

The song is a constant encouragement to drifting marriages with its challenge to seek for openness, growth, and joyous relationship. It also makes an excellent premarital manual. As a biblical perfect example, it brings healing to the core of our being with its hope of covenant love as it reshapes our marriages. Its representation of the covenant love relationship also has application to the covenant love relationship enjoyed by God's church.

GOD'S ORDER AND PURPOSE OF MARRIAGE

Many a husband have failed in growing a godly marriage. A few keys of building a godly marriage have been given in the song of Solomon. Faithfulness, verbal affirmation, friendship, romantic getaways, working through conflict, and availability are but a few. We are to examine Song of Solomon as a God given inspired instructions of a picture of a loving godly marriage. We are invited to reach toward loving godly marriage wholeheartedly taking the example of the beloved husband to praise his bride's (wife's) beauty, appreciate her looks and works. Husband learn to speak the language of love and build up your wife verbally. Verbally express your love to your wife in positive and creative ways. It will cause her to be secure in your relationship and improve your love life. In pure and candid language husband extol your wife. In Solomon's example praise your wife. Tell her:

Song of Solomon 1:8 – Darling, you are fairest among women.

Song of Solomon 1.10 – Your cheeks are lovely with ornaments. Your neck is lovely with chains of gold.

Song of Solomon 1:15 – You see you are fair, my love You have dove's eyes.

Song of Solomon 4:1 - Your hair is like flocks of goats going down from mount Gilead.

Song of Solomon 4:2 – Your teeth *are* like a flock of shorn *sheep* Which have come up from the washing. Every one of which bears twins, and none *is* barren among them.

Song of Solomon 4:3 -Your lips *are* like a strand of scarlet, and your mouth is lovely. Your temples behind your veil *are* like a piece of pomegranate.

Song of Solomon 4:4 - Your neck *is* like the tower of David, built for an armory, on which hang a thousand bucklers, all shields of mighty men.

Song of Solomon 4:5 - Your two breasts *are* like two fawns, Twins of a gazelle, which feed among the lilies.

Song of Solomon 4:7 - You *are* all fair, my love, my wife and *there is* no spot in you. You are altogether beautiful, my love and there is no flaw in you.

Song of Solomon 4:9 - You have ravished my heart my sister, *my* spouse; You have ravished my heart with one *look* of your eyes, with one link of your necklace.

Song of Solomon 4:10 - How fair is your love, my sister, *my* spouse! How much better than wine is your love, and the scent of your perfumes than all spices! Song of Solomon 4:11 - Your lips, O *my* spouse, Drip as the honeycomb; Honey and milk *are* under your tongue. And the fragrance of your garments is like the fragrance of Lebanon.

Song of Solomon 6:4 - O my love, you *are as* beautiful as Tirzah, Lovely as Jerusalem, awesome as *an army* with banners!

Song of Solomon 6:5 - Turn your eyes away from me, for they have overcome me. Your hair *is* like a flock of goats Going down from Gilead.

Song of Solomon 6:6 - Your teeth *are* like a flock of sheep which have come up from the washing. Everyone bears twins, and none is barren among them.

Song of Solomon 6:7 - Your temples behind your veil are like a piece of pomegranate.

Song of Solomon 6:8-9 - There are sixty queens and eighty concubines, and virgins without number. But you My dove, you are the only one, you are my perfect one. You are the only one of your mother. You are the favorite of the one who bore her. The daughters see you and call you blessed. The queens and the concubines, praised you.

Song of Solomon 6:10 – My wife and my love you look forth as the morning, Fair as the moon, Clear as the sun, Awesome as *an army* with banners.

Song of Solomon 7:1 Your feet in sandals are very beautiful. O daughter of Abraham! The curves of your thighs *are* like jewels.

Song of Solomon 7:2 The work of your hands is like the work of the hands of a skillful workman. Your navel *is* a rounded goblet; It lacks no blended beverage.

Your waist *is* a heap of wheat Set about with lilies.

Song of Solomon 7:3 - Your two breasts *are* like two fawns, Twins of a gazelle.

Song of Solomon 7:4 Your neck *is* like an ivory tower, Your eyes *like* the doves. Your nose *is* like the tower of Lebanon which looks toward Damascus.

Song of Solomon 7:5 Your head *crowns* you like *Mount* Carmel, and the hair of your head *is* like purple.

Song of Solomon 7:6 - How fair and how pleasant you are, O love, with your delights!

Song of Solomon 7:7 - This stature of yours is like a palm tree, and your breasts *like* its clusters.

Song of Solomon 7:8 - Your breasts are like clusters of the vine. The fragrance of your breath is like apples

Song of Solomon 7:9 - The roof of your mouth is like the best wine.

Chapter 19

Wife's responsibility in Marriage

The only two people who can come together to become one flesh is a husband (Male man) and a wife (Female man). Holy Matrimony or what is casually known as Wedlock is an office ordained by God, a Holy union, wherein the husband serves the wife and the wife the husband. The worst thing a male man can do is marry the wrong female man and vice versa.

Proverbs 27:15, "On a stormy day drops of rain drive a man out of his house; so also does a railing woman drive a man out of his house."

Nothing can be more miserable than having to spend every day of your life with an evil wife. What does it mean to be a godly woman? If you are married, this is what you must strive to be. If you are not married this is what you must orientate yourself to be. The duties of the wife can be narrowed down to two.

The **first duty** that a good wife must fulfill is helping her husband

becoming his help meet.

In the beginning, when Jehovah made Adam, as the scripture has said in ***Genesis 2:18 KJV. And the L***ORD*** God said, it is not good that the man should be alone; I will make him a help meet for him"* "And *the LORD God said, it is not good that the man should be alone; let us make for him a help suitable to him." NKJV*

He made the female man in Adam to come **alongside** of him, co-responding to him, to work with him, to accomplish the Divine goal or purpose that God has **given** man (male and female). The duty of a good wife, who wants to see a strong marriage and family, is to be the counterpart to her mate in such a way that that which God has given the **both**, she must be by his side as his helper. She is not just another woman on the side, she is an indispensable part of His Divine plan or Purpose.

One of the causes why so many men are miserable and why so many marriages fail is because the wife is not out to help him, she's using the marriage to help herself. She has a faulty view of the relationship. Instead of being his partner and coming alongside to increase their relationship with God, she becomes a part of the opposition, not cooperating with God's agenda for the family, but using it as a launching pad for her own purposes. When a wife loses site that God's first expectation of her in relationship to her husband is to be his helper, then a negative atmosphere is created in the household that is difficult to overcome.

So, the question is, "What does a helper look like?" Now, the assumption, ladies, is that if God expects you to help your husband, the understanding is that your husband needs help! Truthfully, male men are not complete in and of themselves. That is the purpose why God created female men. So, if you are finding fault with your husband, he needs help; and you are the helper. If you are saying, "My husband is messed up!" you are the helper. You cannot complain that he is not what he ought to be if you're not fulfilling your role as the helper! God made you the helper because male man desperately needs help. He desperately needs someone to come alongside who will be different **than** him, to **complete** him, thereby fulfilling the Divine plan of God.

Therefore, whenever the faults of your husband manifests, these are opportunities for you to fulfill your scriptural duty. It is a grievous mistake to pester and curse about how jumbled up your husband is. Instead analyze the kind of helper God has called you to be. In fact, if you are the opposite of your husband, wonderful! That means you are the answer to fill in all the blank spots where he needs help to make up what he is not. That's not an opportunity for revolt, but an opportunity for godly assistance. You are the one to help, mold and shape him into the male that God ultimately wants him to be to carry out the agenda of the household.

Chapter 20

The Worth of a Wife

Proverbs 31 gives the description of a prolific helpmeet. There is more to a wife than meets the eye. She is an excellent virtuous wife, and her worth is far above jewels. The scripture in Proverbs 31 gives her description.

Proverbs 31:10, "Who can find an excellent wife? For her worth is far above jewels." ("Who shall find a virtuous woman? for such a one is more valuable than precious stones."

Many ladies have a low view of themselves which make them a weak wife. When you look at yourself as a priceless diamond, as you are in God's eyes, then you will act accordingly. If you only look at yourself as a substitute jewelry, you are going to live as one. It could be made to look like the real thing, but it's not. Proverbs 31 is talking about the **real Wife**, an authentic wife not a plastic one. Not a wife that is so made up that you don't know what the real thing looks like. And scripture says when a male man finds this kind of a wife, a true and authentic wife, he has got a piece of jewelry that is very valuable. And what is the hallmark of this wife?

Proverbs 31:12, "For she employs all her living for her godly **husband's good**.*"*

She will do him good and not evil all the days of her life. Now if your **godly husband** was asked "**what good is your wife to you?**", would he have an answer? Can he measure how you are constantly, perpetually, determinately looking out for his good? Can he raise the point, if asked the question, that every time this wife wakes up she is thinking about how to make him a better husband? And if that is not your number one agenda item, you are not a godly wife. You may be a bed partner, you may be a cook, you may be this and you may be that, but a good wife seeks the good of her husband all the days of her life. This is conditional to his godly leadership to which you are obligated to submit. That is, just as he is loving and honoring and cherishing you, you are to wake up and ask, "What good can I be to him today?"

Help him In and Out of the House

One of the first ways the excellent virtuous wife helps him is around the house.

Proverbs 31:13-14, "Gathering wool and flax, she makes it serviceable with her hands. She is like a ship trading from a distance: so, she procures her livelihood."

Proverbs 31:16, "She views a farm and buys it: and with the fruits of her hands she plants a possession."

Proverbs 31:24, "She makes fine linens, and sells girdles…"

There is a warped view among some "Christians" that if you are a Christian wife you sit home and throw your college education in the garbage. That way there is no productivity, no skill. But the Proverbs 31 woman is one who is skilled, she saves money, uses money, and spends money wisely. But she's doing this to the good of her husband. This is not like modern women who are building their own career with their own money with their own bank account and they write their own checks. That's not the godly woman. Because a godly woman, while she uses those skills, always brings it back home for the embellishment of the **home** and the enhancement of her **husband**. There should never be monetary competition.

And if you love your career so much that your husband is never benefiting from the career that you love, then you're not a godly wife. You bought the lie that you're your own woman, you do your own thing, and that man is your inconvenience. That is a lie! The feminism movement is born from satanic rebellion against the Holy God. But because many women have established their own bank accounts, and spend their own money for their own agenda, and the good of the husband is nowhere to be found, then the blessings of God will not rest on your life or be in your household. Your godly home will become a godless home.

When you begin to live your married life with no thought of the betterment of your husband, you have joined the adversary in dissolving your marriage. God did not give you a husband for you to still be an independent single woman. He gave you a husband so that you could partner with him, helping him by using your gifts, your skills, and your abilities that He has blessed you with, for the betterment of the whole household. Whenever your career demands negates your duty as wife and mother, you're in the wrong career, and it is not a calling from God.

The Proverbs 31 woman uses her abilities, she does not throw them away. She also helps him parentally.

Help him Parentally

Proverbs 31:15, "And she rises by night and gives food to her household..."

Proverbs 31:21, "Her husband is not anxious about those at home when he tarries anywhere abroad: for all her household are clothed."

In other words, she assists the husband by helping with the children; it is not her duty alone. The husband's duty is to manage the household, but the wife's duty is to help him. She is not to **replace** him, but she is to **help** him. And here we have a woman who is so committed, so dedicated, that she wakes up early before everyone else to make sure that all the bases are covered.

Now, why does God ask the woman to prioritize the household? Because one of her duties is to raise the next generation of godly seed. And if you must leave the house so much that you cannot assist your husband in a significant way, as a parent and guardian of the children, then you're not fulfilling what God has told you to do. That's why the aged women "...teach the young women to be sober, to be lovers of their husbands, to be lovers of their children, to be discreet, chaste, keepers at home, good, obedient to their own husbands, that the word of God be not blasphemed" (Titus 2:4-5).

That's why the younger women marry, bear children, guide the house 1 Timothy 5:14 "*Therefore I desire that the younger widows marry, bear children, manage the house, give no opportunity to the adversary to speak reproachfully.*"

Never let the outside pull of the world keep you from being a dynamic wife and mother. Never let the schedule outside dictate the schedule inside. She also helps him personally.

Help him Personally

Proverbs 31:17, "She strongly girds her loins, and strengthens her arms for work."

Proverbs 31:22, "She makes for her husband clothes of double texture, and garments for herself of fine linen and scarlet."

This woman is looking good! She takes care of herself. We're not talking about some haggard woman here. This man is excited to go to his house. This woman also helps him ministerially.

Help him Ministerialy

Proverbs 31:20, "And she opens her hands to the needy, and reaches out fruit to the poor."

Proverbs 31:26, "But she opens her mouth wisely, and according to law."

She is serving the poor and counseling others. So, she has come alongside his ministry, she is a **partner** with him, sharing her wisdom with him. She doesn't have time to gossip, she is spending too much time devoted to her husband. She doesn't have time to spend all day in front of a soap opera, because she has a man that she must make look good. And how good is this man?

Proverbs 31:11, "The heart of her husband trusts in her…"

Proverbs 31:23, "And her husband becomes a distinguished man in the gates, when he sits in council with the old inhabitants of the land."

Everybody knows who this man is because of this wife. Why? Because his lady made certain it was that way. Other people know him because she makes him look good.

Now, I know what you're saying. "What about me?! I don't always want to be in the background! I don't always want to be hidden! I don't always want to be making some man look good! I want to look good! I want people to talk about me!" Well, if you seek recognition, the bible states the way it should come about.

Proverbs 31:28, "And her kindness to them sets up her children for them, and they grow rich, and her husband praises her."

The husband should praise her and teach his children to praise her. He should teach the children well, so they say, "Thank you, Mom, that on freezing days I'm warm. Thank you, Mom, that on cold days I have hot food." When you have a wife like this you should talk about her all day long. You should say, "Thank you. Can't live without you. I need you. I enjoy you." All the people you meet should know how good your wife is. Go public with wife, don't keep her in the background! There's no privacy here. The wife is to make her husband look good, and the husband is to take his wife public with him.

Submit to your Husband's Godly Leadership

The **second thing** a wife must do is reverence her husband in the Lord only.

Ephesians 5:33, "Nevertheless let every one of you in particular so love his wife even as himself; and the wife see that she reverences her husband."

Ephesians 5:22-24 explains the doctrine of submission. The word "submission" is a good word, but because people have defined it wrongly, you hear of it and disdain it.

Why is it a good word? Because Jesus **submitted himself** to the will of the Father.

First of all, submission has nothing to do with inequality. Submission has to do with accomplishing God's purpose. Jesus submitted to the Father in order to accomplish salvation. He did it for His Father's purpose, never questioning whether it was "fair" or not. It had nothing to do with whether they were equal. 1 Peter 3:7 says a husband and wife are "joint heirs," and therefore equal and are to be treated as **equals**. To submit to your husband does not mean that you are a door mat. It doesn't mean that you are to be pressed on, beaten on, verbally abused using vulgar language, demeaned, or any such thing. You are equal to any man in the eyes of God. But when it comes to His purpose for you, submission in the Lord is absolutely necessary.

To submit to your husband does not mean you agree with him on everything, it means you recognize his position as head of the household to accomplish God's purposes as it relates to the family. You may say, "I can't submit to that man. Preposterous!" You may not agree with everything Mr. Duhuki at your job tells you, but you submit. If you're in court you may not like what the judge thinks, but you submit. We see that these examples have nothing to do with submitting to a man, but submitting to a position.

God has called your husband to a position. His position is head over the household. That's not as a dictator and it's not as "boss man." The job of the head is to give direction to the body. The duty of the wife is to willingly place all of her strengths under the authority of the husband **to FOLLOW HIM AS HE FOLLOWS CHRIST**. That's why it says (and here's some good news for you ladies) at:

Ephesians 5:22, *"Wives, submit yourselves unto your own husbands, as unto the Lord."*

So, you don't have to be concerned about him abusing you! When he leaves or departs from the way of the Lord, he is no longer in the position as your head, he no longer qualifies as the head, for he has abandoned it. That is, you are never to disobey the Lord to follow your husband, because your greater allegiance is to the Lord.

But if this man is trying to serve the Lord, don't work against him. He may not be doing it right, or perfectly, but if the man is trying to please the Lord don't work against him. Why? Because he needs a helper, not a hurter. He needs assistance, not a hindrance. He needs somebody to come alongside and smoothen all those rough edges.

So, every wife should say to her husband, beginning today, "You are my leader. God has put you as head of the household. I am going to honor you as head of the household in the Lord. I am going to follow you as head of the household if you follow Jesus. I'll only ask you, darling, for one thing. Don't lead me away from Christ, because if you lead me away from Christ I'm going to have to leave you and go with my first love. I don't want to leave you and go with my first love, so you follow my first love, so I can follow both of you."

That's the idea! That he follows Christ and you follow him. But ladies, he needs to hear that from you. He needs to hear that you are going to honor and reverence his position as head of the household as he follows Christ. If you can submit to a boss you don't like, then you can submit to a husband you don't like. Because it's not about liking the husband, it's about obeying the Lord. A lot of wives say, "I can't submit!" Well, how do you know? You've never tried! "I can't follow!" How do you know?! He told you one thing that was wrong and now you won't listen to anything?

Many wives have never told their husband that they are willing to come under his authority as he follows Christ to lead the household and motivate him to follow Christ. Rather they work against him by fussing at him, griping at him, and complaining that he never does anything right. It' is like after he gets beaten up outside the household all day long, now he is gotta come home to be beaten up some more. He ought to come home to somebody that will love him, hug him, caress him, affirm him, strengthen him, dignify him, and to a wife who is gonna to recognize that he may not be anybody downtown, but "he is somebody in this house, and I'm gonna make sure he is somebody!" If your attitude is, "My husband is no good," maybe he is no good because nobody is helping him.

That's what headship is. Jesus submitted to the Father, the husband submits to Jesus, the wife submits to the husband using all her gifts and strengths for the betterment of the household. A wife who does not submit herself to her husband has not submitted to God, so don't tell anyone how spiritual you are. You can "go to church" every week, but if your husband does not know that you recognize his position as head then you are a carnal woman. You can read your bible every day, have devotions, go to bible study every Wednesdays, and still be out of the will of God if you don't honor your husband in the Lord.

For some wives, their husband may not know how to be a good husband because he was not raised by a good father; has perhaps never seen a godly husband. Not knowing what a godly husband is, he will therefore have to learn. It may take some time, and these wives may have to humble themselves and say, "Father, I have sinned in this area. I have not been a helper, I've been a hurter. I confess that I've sinned, and today I'm going to tell my husband that he now has a helper. Someone who is going to work **with** him, not **against** him. Someone who is going to **support** him, not **crucify** him. So, what are you to do? Read 1 Peter 3:1-6.

Ungodly Husbands

1 Peter 3:1, "Likewise, ye wives, be in subjection to your own husbands; that, if any obey not the word, they also may without the word be won by the conversation of the wives;"

The scripture now raises a question about wives whose husbands have erred from the Way. The world says, "Wife! You don't need him…leave! You don't have to go through that! Walk out!" That's not what scripture says. Now who are you going to believe? Are you going to believe your "friends," or are you going to believe the Word of God? And that's the problem. There are too many wives listening to too many wrong voices. God says if your husband is not a godly man yet, he can still be won without a word, but by the **behavior** of the wife! God didn't call you to be your husband's pastor. He didn't call you to preach to him. He didn't call you to be his nag. The way a messed-up husband is won is not by the preaching skill of his wife. If you have noticed, the more you try to change him with your voice, the worse he gets. And you know why? Because you're dealing with the one thing that no man will compromise on, and that's his ego. A man will let you mess with a lot, but what he will not let you mess with is his ego. Men have fought and killed since the beginning of time for their ego!

So, what does the Lord want you to do when it comes to dealing with the husband's ego? He wants you to get out of the way, so He can chastise him. God says be like Jesus in the same way. Now what was Jesus like?

1 Peter 2:22-23, "*Who did no sin, neither was guile found in his mouth: Who, when he was reviled, reviled not again; when he suffered, he threatened not;*"

Have you tried God's way to help your husband, or have you been fussing for years? Because if you have been fussing for years, you have been asking God not to help him, that you will take care of it yourself.

You should make your husband stare at you and wonder, "What has gotten into you?" when you ask your husband, "What can I do for you today?" When he comes home and he sees this haggard, burned-out, no-makeup looking wife, who looked good for Mr. Duhuki all day, and now he's got to hear, "Yea, I'm tired. What do you want to eat?! I bought some milk, there's some cereal, go get it yourself." No, it should be more like, "Honey, what can I cook for you today? What would you like to eat? How can I take care of you? How can I look good for you?" And he is supposed to stare and say, "Huh?"

Shock him with your help and your submission. Make him stare. Make him wonder what went wrong. Make him say, "Wow, I like this." Now, you are probably saying, "You don't know my husband. He's going to take advantage of that." God says, "You leave that to me." He's asking you to trust in Him. As your husbands observe your chaste, holy and respectful behavior, they may be won.

1 Peter 3:3-4, *"Whose adorning let it not be that outward adorning of plaiting the hair, and of wearing of gold, or of putting on of apparel; But let it be the hidden man of the heart, in that which is not corruptible, even the ornament of a meek and quiet spirit, which is in the sight of God of great price."*

Wives spend a lot of time making themselves look good on the outside, but God says, that more importantly, make yourself good on the inside. There's no point in looking beautiful on the outside if you're ugly on the inside. So be beautiful on the inside!

Language is Important

In Genesis 24, Rebekah was able to meet God's divine appointment for her life (marriage) because she was faithfully carrying out her current obligations. She had a ready willingness to serve others. These qualities put her in the right place at the right time with the right attitude when God intended to match her with Isaac. Isaac's servant asked for some water from her, *"And she said, Drink,* **my lord***..."* (Genesis 24:18). She reverenced a stranger, and God used that stranger to bring Rebekah and Isaac in marriage.

Here Is another example

1 Peter 3:6, *"Even as Sara obeyed Abraham,* **calling him lord***:"* Sara reverenced her husband. How do you know? Because of how she talked to him. She said, "lord." Now, look at your husband and say, "lord." Practice it and say, "lord." Take it one step further and say, "My lord." In other words, her submission was not private, but universal. "Lord!"

In Genesis 18:12, she calls Abraham, "lord." God told her that in one year from now, she's going to get pregnant, *"...Therefore Sarah laughed within herself, saying, After I am waxed old shall I have pleasure, my* **lord** *being old also?"* (Genesis 18:12).

What's the point? Sara was in an impossible situation, being 90 years old, her husband's 100, no pregnancy in sight, but she called him lord. And when God saw her reverence Abraham, Abraham could do things he couldn't do before, and Sara got pregnant! When she called him lord, God did something to him. If you reverence your husband, God can make him do things he can't do otherwise. God can turn his attitude around and his life around, if you do your part; if you get out of the way so God can dispense His loving chastisement and Grace.

So, reverence your husband; lift him up, embellish him, serve him, while he does the same for you.

Chapter 21

The Divine Order to Marriage

In Genesis *2:18, 21-22* we read:

And the Lord God said, "It is not good for the man to be alone. I will make a helper suitable for him." . . . So, the Lord God caused the man to fall into a deep sleep; and while he was sleeping, He took one of the man's ribs and closed the place with flesh. Then the Lord God made a woman from the rib (side) he had taken out of the man, and he brought her to the man.

Many questions are asked like - Why did God do it that way? Why create one being and then take a part of that being and create a second, differentiated yet complementary being who is "bone of his bones and flesh of his flesh," a being who is sexually, emotionally and in other ways different, yet of his own substance? Upon seeing Eve, Adam could have observed, "It's me . . . but not me." Well, if you think about it, it does sound like the kind of thing you might expect a Trinity to do.

The Trinity (Father, Son, Holy Spirit) is a family, and thus man in God's image must be made a family as well. Therefore, a man cannot completely realize the essence of his existence until he learns to exist with someone and for someone. Both relationship and communion are crucial to this process.

Therefore, we see from Genesis 1 and 2 that God made the woman from the side of the man so that the man would not be alone. New Testament teaches that saints have since discovered that He also created the Church from the side of the second Adam Christ for the same reason of intimate fellowship.

The reason the male man is to marry a female man is because female man was originally a constituent part of the man (male and female), she must return to become one with him again, so that the full expression and design of God's image in human beings can be revealed.

Here we have another parallel between the Old Testament type and the New Testament fulfillment. Eve was to reunite with her source and become one with him—just as we are with Christ, as He prayed in John 17. Sexuality, therefore, is a prefigurement of the intimate relationship that God desires to have with man. In fact, the marital union and covenant in all its dimensions is meant to gloriously reveal the very image of God in ways that we can only begin to understand.

There is more to this mystery than can be seen on the surface. The union of a man and a woman in Holy Matrimony is not literally the permanent recombining of two bodies into one. This is mystery that reaches depths of meaning beyond what our present intellectual capacity can grasp.

What a female is as a part of man (Male and female) is not tied to individuated pieces of flesh and bone but is far broader and more profound than meets the eye. She is the necessary compliment to him that together reveals the glory of the image of God in humanity. Her parts and his parts each have their own order and function. Together and rightly ordered, their united differences ignite the power and glory of creation itself, which is the consummate activity of God from the beginning.

Therefore, God does a two-stage creation of man. First, he makes the male man and female man. Then in phase two, God removes the female from man side and makes Eve a separate being, though of Adam's substance, designed to ultimately reunite to her source through the mystery of Holy Matrimony.

The power of that union is meant to gloriously reveal the very image of God to angels and archangels and all the company of heaven and earth. That is why Satan fights tooth and nail to pervert and distort rightly ordered human sexuality, holy matrimony, the family, and fatherhood in particular.

In fact, the amount of time and effort that Satan expends to destroy the image of God reflected in marriage, fatherhood and human sexuality is a benchmark or yardstick of just how incredibly important it is to God's plan and the expression of His glory.

Friends, there is a profound reason for the way God ordered the creation of man. The one that is observed throughout Scripture and one that we must conform to if we are to find the fulfillment of our very being as humans. It is ordered as the union of a male man and a female woman in marriage, heterosexual and monogamous, an order that Jesus unambiguously reaffirmed in the gospels.

The Lord might well think some of the same thoughts as Romeo as he waited outside Juliet's bedroom balcony for the slightest glimmer of hope that she shared in his love for her. God may see us at a worship service, erupting with a sudden burst of romantic sentiment as we sing our love songs to Him.

"But soft, what light through yonder window breaks," He might exclaim. "It is my lady. Oh, it is my love. Oh, that she knew she were."

But so often, His hope is dashed as we leave the service and return to our self-involved lives without putting any of those sentiments into practice—without any change in our lives, without any deepening of our pursuit of Him, without any reality beyond the sentimental notions of those love songs that we mouthed.

Christ has made promises and sworn and faithfully executed oaths to bind Himself to us and to bind evil and cast it off, if we will simply be true to Him in ways that are real.

Eph 5:32, is speaking of a male man and female man becoming one flesh, Paul says: *"This is a profound mystery—but I am talking about Christ and the Church."*

The veil is removed that had hidden the answer to the mystery of the supreme purpose and end for God having saved us, as well as the mysteries behind God having made us male and female, sexual beings, called into faithful, monogamous, heterosexual relationships that were to personify the virtue of sacrificial love.

Genesis and Ephesians helps us understand that there is both a corporate and individual "mystical marriage "between Christ and believers. We have direct experience of this reality through dreams and visions.

This is why Satan is targeting defacing and destroying human sexuality and marriage. He is trying to mock God. He is trying to mar the very image of God expressed on this earth through the marital bond, sexual and otherwise. His plan is to rob God of His deepest and most passionate purpose of marital union with man. Satan knows if he can destroy the beauty of the earthly bond, he can destroy in us any desire for the heavenly bond.

We were created to live in marital union with God, both now and in the age to come. Everything about a healthy marital union on this earthly realm has been designed by God to reflect the interaction that we are meant to have with God Himself.

Why Marriage Matters for Adults

Marriage has a much greater impact in our lives than many have assumed. This is especially true in the area of adult health and well-being. A good marriage is both men's and women's best bet for living a long and healthy life. *Why Married People are Happier, Healthier, and Better Off Financially?* Husbands and wives who are in their first marriages, on average, enjoy significantly higher levels of physical and mental health than those who are either single, divorced or living together. All things considered, *Married people are happier than unmarried ones of the same age. People who are married not only have higher incomes and enjoy greater emotional support, they tend to be healthier. Married people live longer than unmarried ones.*

Chapter 22

Spiritual Husbands Or Wives

What you know about Spiritual Husbands or Wives will determine your destiny in life. Spiritual husband and wife is a very deep spiritual issue that are kept away from millions of Christians today. Spiritual husbands are specially commissioned by Satan to molest, trouble, and scatter good and godly homes, relationships, and life in general. I pray that Jehovah will open your understanding on this matter, in Jesus name.

Spiritual husbands and wives are spiritual enemies living and sleeping with one. They are very stubborn, aggressive and dangerous. They are terrible enemies with killer motives to kill your joy, peace, health, mind, will, emotions, attitudes, calling, virtue, marriage. Often times they do not need permission as they violate the right of their victims, molest their victims with sex in the dream. They are desperate and very wicked. They can enter and start manifesting in one's life through various means which include, sexual immorality, Pornography, Spirit wife and or husband can be inherited. They can enter one's life by evil dedication of the individual, underwear manipulation, through tattooing and incision.

Signs of Spirit Husband or Wife

Signs of spirit husband and wife include Sexual relationships in dreams, hatred of marriage, being ditched by serious partners, missing one's menstrual period in the dream, pregnancy in the dream, breast-feeding a baby in the dream, having a family in the dream, shopping with another male man or female man in the dream who is not your husband or wife, seeing another man sleeping by one's side in the dream, or Sudden Hatred by earthly spouse. Serious gynecological problems, having a miscarriage after sexual dreams, Dream marriages, Constant wet dreams, late marriage or no marriage at all.

Praying the word of God will set one free from this oppressive, binding and embarrassing evil spirit.

Prayer

1. Spirit husband / wife, I declare to you, my body is the temple of God therefore you do not have control over my body
2. Spirit husband/spirit wife; release me now, in the name of Jesus.
3. Every spirit husband/wife, I divorce you by the blood of Jesus.
4. Every spirit wife/every spirit husband, die, in the name of Jesus.
5. Everything you have deposited in my life, come out by fire, in the name of Jesus.
6. Every power that is working against my marriage, fall down and die, in the name of Jesus.
7. I divorce and renounce my marriage with the spirit husband or wife, in the name of Jesus.
8. I break all covenants entered into with the spirit husband or wife, in the name of Jesus.
9. I command the thunder fire of God to burn to ashes the wedding gown, ring, photographs and all other materials used for the marriage, in Jesus' name.
10. I send the fire of God to burn to ashes the marriage certificate, in the name of Jesus.
11. I break every blood and soul-tie covenants with the spirit husband or wife, in the name of Jesus.

12. I reject the children born to the marriage, in Jesus' name.
13. I withdraw my blood, sperm or any other part of my body deposited on the altar of the spirit husband or wife, in Jesus name.
14. You spirit husband or wife tormenting my life and earthly marriage I bind you with hot chains and fetters of God and cast you out of my life into the deep pit, and I command you not to ever come into my life again, in the name of Jesus.
15. I return to you, every property of yours in my possession in the spirit world, including the dowry and whatsoever was used for the marriage and covenants, in the name of Jesus.
16. I drain myself of all evil materials deposited in my body as a result of our sexual relation, in Jesus' name.
17. Lord, send Holy Ghost fire into my root and burn out all unclean things deposited in it by the spirit husband or wife, in the name of Jesus.

Chapter 23

Unbelieving Spouses

In the church of Jesus Christ many women grieve the fact their husbands have not made commitment to Christ and their marriage relationship. This recalls 1 Corinthians 7:13-14

¹³ And a woman who has a husband who does not believe, if he is willing to live with her, let her not divorce him. ¹⁴ For the unbelieving husband is sanctified by the wife, and the unbelieving wife is sanctified by the husband; otherwise your children would be unclean, but now they are holy.

The scriptures bring the understanding that when a man is pleased to dwell with his saved wife he is sanctified by the faith of the wife. The word (pleased) contextually means – the husband fulfills his role of stewarding faithfulness to his wife. He loves, provides, and protects his wife. Not a user, abuser, oppressor, hater, self – centered, self – conceited, and egocentric. We are saved by faith. Those two being one in God's eyes means the faith of the wife is imputed to the husband. This is an amazing, intriguing and provocative concept. The Old Testament states that when clean and unclean meet, the result was the clean because the unclean became clean. In the new Testament, now that we are sanctified by the blood of Jesus and not that of animals perhaps the unclean husband is made clean by the faith of the wife. How possible can this be?

Jesus said, "in as much as you have done it unto one of the least of these my disciples, you have done it unto me. "Is it possible that God counts a man who is faithful to his wife as being faithful to meeting His needs? Absolutely!

One thing is sure. The children of a believer are sanctified and the union that brought them forth is also clean. The best explanation of what this means for the unbeliever is, if they are faithful in doing what they know to do for their mate it will be accounted to them as unto the Lord. If they are married to, but despise their mate, will the same be accounted to them? I suppose not.

This knowledge should encourage and liberate husbands and wives from the drivenness to get their partner saved before they die. Salvation is God's work and the best way given a woman to save her husband is through her meek and humble conduct, which does not require a salvation message to be preached.

Let us read Verses 13, 14 in the context of the whole statement 1 Corinthians 7:12-17

12 But to the rest speak I, not the Lord: If any brother hath a wife that believeth not, and she be pleased to dwell with him, let him not put her away. 13And the woman which hath an husband that believeth not, and if he be pleased to dwell with her, let her not leave him. 14 For the unbelieving husband is sanctified by the wife, and the unbelieving wife is sanctified by the husband; otherwise your children would be unclean, but now they are holy. 15 But if the unbeliever departs, let him depart; a brother or a sister is not under bondage in such *cases*. But God has called us to peace. 16 For how do you know, O wife, whether you will save *your* husband? Or how do you know, O husband, whether you will save *your* wife? 17 But as God has distributed to each one, as the Lord has called each one, so let him walk.

Paul is addressing married couples, either husband or wife is saved and the other is not. He preached the Gospel to them and those who got saved are the ones he is teaching at this point. Some are now living in relationships where their wives or husbands did not get saved. Paul is telling them that as long as their unbelieving spouse is pleased to live with them, their marriage is sanctified as holy in the eyes of God, otherwise their children would be unclean. The "Unbelieving Spouse is Sanctified by the Believing Spouse. If the unbelieving spouse leaves the relationship, then the believing spouse is not bound by the laws, and vows of that marriage. Because we do not know if the unbelieving spouse will ever come to the Lord.

In 2 Co 6:14 expounds on what our relationships should be with non-believers. "Be ye not unequally yoked together with unbelievers: for what fellowship hath righteousness with unrighteousness? and what communion hath light with darkness?"

Amos 3:3 puts it this way "Can two walk together, except they be agreed?" Therefore, we can then take both 2 Corinthians 6:14 and Amos 3:3 to mean, a Christian should not ever marry a non-believer.

Finally, concerning having a spouse in heaven, Jesus was asked this question, His answer was in *Matthew 22:29-30- "Jesus answered and said unto them, Ye do err, not knowing the scriptures, nor the power of God. For in the resurrection they neither marry, nor are given in marriage, but are as the angels of God in heaven.*

God Is Absolute Truth

The bible in *John 8:32 declares that "And you will know the truth, and the truth will set you free."*

John 17:17-18 - God desires that ALL of us may know the truth and be set free from men's traditions and opinions and religious dogma. The Truth is the Word of God. It sets free, Truth sanctifies.

[17] Sanctify them by Your truth. Your word is truth. [18] As You sent Me into the world, I also have sent them into the world. Truth purifies 1

Peter 1:22 ² Since you have purified your souls in obeying the truth through the Spirit[a] in sincere love of the brethren, love one another fervently with a pure heart. Truth establishes Ephesians 4:15 ¹⁵ but, speaking the truth in love, may grow up in all things into Him who is the head—Christ. The Spirit compels you to marry the person of Truth's choice . You are free to marry whoever you choose, however make surer the Truth is joining you to your significant one.

Chapter 24

The Unmarried

To those considering to be married read again what the Spirit of grace is saying! 2 Corinthians 6:14-18 - Do not be unequally yoked together with unbelievers. For what fellowship has righteousness with LAWLESSNESS? And what communion has light with DARKNESS? And what accord has Christ with BELIAL (Satan)? Or what part has a believer with an UNBELIEVER? And what agreement has the temple of God with IDOLS? For you are the temple of the Living God. As God has said: "I will dwell in them and walk among them. I will be their God, and they shall be my people. Therefore, come out from among them and be separate, says the Lord. DO NOT touch what is unclean and I will receive you. I will be a Father to you, and you shall be My sons and daughters, says the Lord Almighty."

Isaiah 55:8,9 - For My thoughts are not your thoughts nor are your ways My ways" says the Lord. For as the heavens are higher than the earth, so are My ways higher than your ways & My thoughts than your thoughts.

Unbelieving Spouse

Certainly, we are not to be married to an unbelieving person. In my counseling sessions, I hear spouses who had all good intentions for marriage lament regretfully that they didn't heed the many warnings and God's biding not to marry that individual. They leaned on their own understanding, emotions, traditions and counsel of uninformed people hence the destruction of their entire lives. People who get married to unbelievers will change back, it is only a matter of time and backslide or live in misery because of all kind of abuses.

The devil works triple time to their detriment until they decide it is not worthy anymore living the Christian life. The only choice they have is to work out their soul salvation. If it is not working it won't work. There is nothing to hold it together. so even though God hates divorce, they would rather leave and remarry a believer.

Walking by sight is making decisions based on emotions which is deceptive. Emotions are temporary and marriage based on emotions has no foundation and great will be its fall. Marriage that will stand the wiles of the enemy is the one founded on the Truth and worked out by Truth. The bible in **2 Timothy 2:19 Nevertheless the solid foundation of God stands sure, having this seal: "The Lord knows those who are His," and, "Let everyone who names the name of Christ[a] depart from iniquity."** That which is not of faith is sin. Iniquity or sin is the one that destroys foundations of marriages. Marriages founded on the solid foundation of the word of God cannot be moved. Faith comes by hearing the word of God. And the word of God is Truth **Psalm 33:4(NKJV) For the word of the LORD *is* right, and all His work *is done* in truth.**

Chapter 25

Divorce

Today, it is very common to hear certain people are contemplating divorce, filing for divorce or are divorced without considering the serious damaging consequences Divorce has not only to the divorcees, but to the whole society.

The process of divorce is a dark cold road that enrages or steams up bitter envy (feelings), strife, offense, stirs up tense emotions and provokes people to commit detrimental acts that they would not have otherwise committed. This is the harmful sin commonly committed by spouses once they are in the throes of divorce. Sometimes it is aimed at dispensing their own brand of vengeance, to somehow gain sympathy, and or to gain the upper hand in their divorce court proceedings.

The Root cause of Bitterness

To some of the spouses, the sting of divorce implants a bitter seed deep into their hearts. Once that seed germinates, these men and women are subject, not only to hurt others, but to injure themselves by committing irrevocable self-inflicted wounds. Some men become avowed women haters and turn to abusing and exploiting the female gender. They become so bitter against marriage that they go on a one-man mission to persuade other men to never get married. These men are the originators of the current male marriage strike. Others engage in indiscriminate sex, commit suicide or turn to homosexuality. Others become so bitter, that they get a vasectomy. They vow never to give another woman the opportunity to hurt them after their vindictive *ex*-wives used the court to take their children from their lives.

Some females become so bitter that they engage in no holds barred male bashing. To these females, all males are dogs and they passionately convey that message to every female who crosses their path. These females join the ranks of other fuming feminists whose mission in life is to emasculate the male gender. They glory in the fact that they frequently succeed at eroding true masculinity and castrating real manhood. Their mantra (commonly repeated phrase) is "Whatever a male can do, we can do better!" Other females resort to promiscuity, lesbianism, or turn to drugs and alcohol to bandage the pain caused by their divorce. Still others reduce themselves to willfully committing vengeful acts such as paternity (fatherhood) fraud and marital fraud.

Vicious Child Custody Battles

At the parent's behest, innocent children become nervous, get fidgety and tears roll down their cheeks crying profusely and muttering statements such as, "I wished my parents would stop fighting, I can't take this anymore," and "Why can't we be a normal family?" In that moment of anguish and hurt they yearn for somebody to console them. The precious children become victims of their parent's nasty divorce and a casualty of their vicious child custody battle. Child custody battles have become the norm in our divorce prone societies. Innocent children are forced into the fury as they are coaxed, coerced and or bribed into choosing sides between parents. The overflow of hostilities between the divorcing spouses will most likely leave deep emotional, psychological and social scars on the child's life.

The Child Becomes a Pawn

Some spouses use their child as a pawn (Instrument) to exact vengeance against their *ex*-spouse. Ex-Spouses who have had a child together, after their split, although have joint custody, one agrees to allow their child to live with their *ex*-spouse. Years later when the one with custody remarries, the other becomes so furious that they go back to court and file for full custody! By this time their child is doing great in school, had adjusted to his or her stepparent and displays no behavioral problems. The custody drama becomes extremely strenuous because their child adored his or her stepparent, loves their home, and cherishes his or her neighborhood friends.

Members from the three families of the ex-spouses and the new spouse's family all plead with the plaintiff ex-spouse not to drag the families through the court. Plaintiff ex-spouse refuses to relent! He or she remains adamant about obtaining full custody and forcing his or her *ex*-spouse to start paying him or her child support. Finally, the plaintiff ex-spouse wins full custody and immediately removes their child from his or her stable household and familiar environment. That is when the child's life changes for the worse.

In the child's new home, there is no stability. His or her new custodian parent has various opposite gender friends and while the new custodian parent is out on dates, leaves child the remote control and microwave dinners. The home alone child begins spending most of his or her time watching music videos, and inappropriate Tv programs. Consequently, the child's grades take a nose dive. He or she starts displaying behavioral problems such as disrespecting his teachers and skipping school. Things escalate when he or she joins a gang and eventually start using drugs and get in promiscuity. While his or her life spirals out of control, the new custodian parent refuses to call the other child's parent and under no circumstances does the new custodian parent want his or her child communicating with his or her stepfather or stepmother. Custodian parent further prevents other child's parent from attending his or her scheduled court ordered visits with his or her other parent.

In the end, their son or daughter drops out of school and is arrested on charges stemming from a gang related burglary. After the judge adds up the aggravating sentencing factors, ranging from high school dropout, gang member, burglary, drug abuser, the teenager is given years of sentence in an adult prison. The new custodian parent's evil plot works out to perfection!

Abuse and Domestic Violence

The stress of a failing marriage inflames some spouses to retaliate in an unorthodox, irregular or maverick manner. They resort to committing abuse and violence. Their bitterness causes them to wield or exert the weapons of abuse and domestic violence against their spouses, children and family members, and against the opposite gender. These men and women literally become human ticking time bombs.

Generational Curse

It goes without saying that divorce tears apart the fundamental basis of a child's security of having both their father and mother in their life. When a child becomes a victim of divorce, oftentimes, they take on the generational curse of divorce themselves. They in turn pass this curse on to their children. In some families, the curse of divorce runs four and five or more generations deep. If you searched his or her family lineage, you will find no one who has had a stable marriage, or who knows what a healthy marriage looks like.

Parental Alienation Syndrome

Parental Alienation Syndrome (PAS) is when hurt and embittered parents poison their children against their spouses. These parents barrage or onslaught their adolescents, teenagers and adult children with a mixture of lies, false allegations and constant criticisms. Their intention is to persuade their child to hate or despise their other parent.

Parentification of Children

Some parents spin into an emotional downward spiral during or after their marital rupture. Emotionally, they become incapable of dealing with the realities of their divorce. When that happens, the parents expect, and in many cases, demand that their children behave as adults. The parent-child relationship is annulled and is replaced with a psychologically damaging (*child replaces parent*) relationship. The children are forced to take care of their moms or dads. They become the primary caretakers of their siblings and usually run the households. They provide their parents with a false sense of emotional security. Some parents use their children to meet their need for intimacy. Parents sleep with their children, (*not sexually*) just to have a shoulder to cry on, to have someone to hold and someone to talk to. They talk to their children about their problems and issues, sharing with them details that children should be shielded from. In turn, these children don't get a chance to properly develop emotionally, and usually become dysfunctional marriage partners.

It is an undeniable fact that divorce is stressful, painful and harmful, but it does not mean the end of your life. With God's help, you can regroup, recover and move on. The deadly sins of divorce do not mean that you should stay in a harmful, abusive or violent marriage. A thousand times NO! If you have found yourself booby trapped in an abusive, violent or harmful marriage, to be blunt, getting out may be your only recourse to regaining your sanity, physical safety and peace of mind nothing missing, lacking or broken. I pray that you seek proper godly counsel and make the right decision.

Chapter 26

God-Honoring Marriage

The Bible is an equal opportunity exasperator or aggravator. It convicts of sin people who are not, yet Jesus followers and it irritates people who are Jesus followers when they miss the mark. Jesus followers' life is not always flawless. Sometimes there is graphic brutality and violence. Sometimes there is strong language and profanity. Sometimes there is nudity and sex and other adult themes. At least Jesus knows these are there in your marriages. And the Bible talks to real people, who are trying to manage real life God's way. So, if we are going to study the Bible and learn about doing life with God, God's way, from His Word, we are going to run into somethings from time to time which will embarrass us. This is true because if we don't talk about the alligators, people will keep walking around missing an arm, or a leg. Marriage is the deepest, and the richest, and the most complex of all human relationships. It is the only place where God expects all the different forms of love to be explored to the fullest.

God's Love and Joy is Perfected by abiding in His **love.** Let us read what God says about love.

John 15:9 says, *"As the Father **love**d Me, I also have **love**d you; abide in My **love**.*

John 17:23 *I in them, and You in Me; that they may be made **perfect** in one, and that the world may know that You have sent Me, and have **love**d them as You have **love**d Me.*

Colossians 3:14 But above all these things put on **love**, which is the bond of **perfect**ion.

1 John 2:5 *But whoever keeps His word, truly the **love** of God is **perfect**ed in him. By this we know that we are in Him.*

1 John 4:12 *Seeing God Through **Love** No one has seen God at any time. If we **love** one another, God abides in us, and His **love** has been **perfect**ed in us.*

1 John 4:17 *The Consummation of **Love**] **Love** has been **perfect**ed among us in this: that we may have boldness in the day of judgment; because as He is, so are we in this world.*

1 John 4:18 *There is no fear in **love**; but **perfect love** casts out fear, because fear involves torment. But he who fears has not been made **perfect** in **love**.* with the grave, the barren womb, and the earth that is not s

Watch this now, in Proverbs 30:15-33 the leech has two daughters—Give and Give! Likewise, it sounds to me like Eros love has two sons get and get never gives! It is never satisfied, it never says, "Enough. It can only be equated satisfied with water and the fire that never says, "Enough!" Those who mock the Father's word, and scorn obedience to His word, and refuse to retain God in their knowledge, they will be given over to a reprobate mind, to do those things which are not convenient. They end up **changing the truth of God into a lie, and worship and serve the creature more than the Creator who is blessed forever. For this reason, God gives them up unto vile affections. The women change the natural use into that which is against nature. Likewise, also the men, leaving the natural use of the woman, burned in their lust one toward another; men with**

men working that which is unseemly, and receiving in themselves that recompense of their error which is meet.

[28] And even as they did not like to retain God in their knowledge, God gave them over to a reprobate mind, to do those things which are not convenient; [29] Being filled with all unrighteousness, fornication, wickedness, covetousness, maliciousness; full of envy, murder, debate, deceit, malignity; whisperers, [30]Backbiters, haters of God, despiteful, proud, boasters, inventors of evil things, disobedient to parents. [20] This *is* the way of an adulterous woman: She eats and wipes her mouth, and says, "I have done no wickedness." [21] For three *things* the earth is perturbed, Yes, for four it cannot bear up: [22] For a servant when he reigns, A fool when he is filled with food,[23] A hateful *woman* when she is married, And a maidservant who succeeds her mistress [24] There are four *things which* are little on the earth, But they *are* exceedingly wise: [25] The ants *are* a people not strong, Yet they prepare their food in the summer; [26] The rock badgers[b] are a feeble folk, Yet they make their homes in the crags; [27] The locusts have no king, Yet they all advance in ranks; [28] The spider[c] skillfully grasps with its hands, And it is in kings' palaces. [29] There are three *things which* are majestic in pace, Yes, four *which* are stately in walk: [30] A lion, *which is* mighty among beasts And does not turn away from any;[31] A greyhound, A male goat also, And a king *whose* troops *are* with him.

[32] If you have been foolish in exalting yourself, Or if you have devised evil, *put your* hand on *your* mouth. [33] For *as* the churning of milk produces butter, And wringing the nose produces blood, So the forcing of wrath produces strife.

The second is Phileo love. Phileo love is friendship love. Friendship love happens when two people love something else together. It's the kind that is of a common passion and common quest or pursuit. We pursue something together, we build something together. For us Jesus' followers, we are to build our marriage together with God on His word. By *Laboring with Lord on His word we Prosper with Him.* Unless we permit the Lord to build our marriage with us we labor

GOD'S ORDER AND PURPOSE OF MARRIAGE

in vain without His word getting involved in building it we found them. We do this by building each other and permitting the Lord to work in us both to will and for to do His good pleasure. (Philippians 2:13 The Lord is not slack concerning His promise, as some count slackness, but is longsuffering toward us, not willing that any should perish but that all should come to repentance.)

By the grace of God which was given to us and as wise master **builders** we must lay the word of God as the foundation. Unless we permit the Lord to guard our marriage with His word, we stay awake in vain. (Psalm 127:1)

Jesus' followers' primary mission in marriage is to hand our spouse back to God better than we got them. The mission is accomplished when we present our spouses to the father more God loving and more Godlike and when each one of us build on it. We must each **one of us** take heed how we **build** our marriage on it. 1 Cor 3:10.

We must go out of our way and preach to our everywhere (soul and body), the Lord working with *us* and confirming the word through the accompanying signs of God-honoring marriage. (Mark 16:20).

Working out Phileo love relationship is the reason we shall hear Jesus say to us at the heaven's gate *Matthew 25:21 Well done,* ***good and faithful servants****: you were* ***faithful*** *over working out your marriage soul salvation, I will make you ruler over many things. Enter into the joy of your lord.*

Another kind of love relationship is Eros love. Eros love relationship fades from time to time and cannot be trusted. Eros love is the kind of love relationship most people think is the heart of marriage. It's not! It is temporary, and you cannot build marriage on it. Marriage built on Eros love relationship is building on the earth without a foundation, against which when the storms pound on it, the floods arise against it, the stream beat vehemently against it will immediately it will fall. And the ruin of that marriage will be great.

Somebody smarter than me once said that money and sex are the two things everybody wants, but nobody in church wants to talk about them. I will rephrase that and say money and sex are the two things the carnally minded gravitate, but none gets contented with them. In Song of Solomon 5:2 *In the Shulamite's Troubled Evening the Shulamite says based on feelings or lust of the flesh; I sleep, but my heart is awake; It is the voice of my beloved! He knocks, saying, "Open for me, my sister, my **love**, my dove, my **perfect** one; For my head is covered with dew, My locks with the drops of the night."*

This kind is short lived. It is based on feelings which come and fade away instantaneously. It is more of fulfilment of fleshly lusts than anything else. Please read with me additional verses what the scriptures records.

John 6:63 It is the Spirit who gives life; the flesh profits nothing... What God is saying is that we are not to be controlled by feelings or lust of the flesh, but we are to have self-control, a people of strong convictions on God's word.

Romans 13:13-14 Let us walk properly, as in the day, not in revelry and drunkenness, not in lewdness and lust, not in strife and envy. But put on the Lord Jesus Christ, and make no provision for the **flesh**, to **fulfill** its **lust**s.

Galatians 5:16 Walk in the Spirit, and you shall not **fulfill** the **lust** of the **flesh**.

Ephesians 2:1-3 By Grace through Faith He made you alive, who were dead in trespasses and sins, in which you once walked according to the course of this world, according to the prince of the power of the air, the spirit who now works in the sons of disobedience, among whom also we all once conducted ourselves in the lusts of our flesh, fulfilling the desires of the flesh and of the mind, and were by nature children of wrath, just as the others.

Eros love is feeling love, romantic love, erotic, sexual love. Eros is incredibly important to a good, God-honoring marriage. However, it can also be incredibly destructive. So, we need to give it some attention and tread carefully. In the wedding of God-honoring marriage the bride and the groom aren't really making promises to each other, they are making promises to God. This is the vertical part of a wedding that the priest (one performing the wedding) asks them, for God: "Will you love each other, comfort each other, honor and keep each other, in sickness and in health and, forsaking all others; giving up all others, renouncing the pursuit of all others, will you be faithful to each other so long as you both shall live?" In other words, what they are saying is "I promise you, God, I will not give my body to any other person no matter what my heart says to me." Now that is a big promise and not hard to keep because when grace and faith is given the opportunity to function in the relationship we are no longer working it by our own abilities. The grace of God which is God's enabling power kicks in and appropriately loves through us. We know that Faith speaks what it believes.

2 Corinthians 4:13 And since we have the same spirit of faith, according to what is written, "I believed and therefore I spoke" Therefore we speak what we want to see or happen. When the soon to become husband and wife couple say to each other we will love each other, comfort each other, honor and keep each other, forsaking all others; giving up all others, renouncing the pursuit of all others, we will be faithful to each other so long as we both shall live." They are declaring and decreeing in agreement with God's word that it is to them what God has declared in His word.

Mary declared in Luke 1:38 Then Mary said, "Behold the maidservant of the Lord! Let it be to me according to your word." Immediately the power of God kicked in and God's plan for mankind redemption became possible.

God says to Paul in Acts 27:23- 24 For there stood by me this night an angel of the God to whom I belong and whom I serve, [24] saying 'Do not be afraid, Paul; you must be brought before Caesar; and indeed, God has granted you all those who sail with you.' In Acts 27:25 - Paul declares what God had told him. "Therefore, take heart, men, for I believe God that it will be just as it had told me." Also, God's delivering grace became available delivering Paul and his compony from destruction.

God Himself declares in Isaiah 55:11 So shall My word be that goes forth from My mouth; It shall not return to Me void, but it shall accomplish what I please, and it shall prosper *in the thing* for which I sent it. This promise becomes possible when the believer sends back to God the word He has spoken. The believer is the one who returns the word of God to Him by declaring on earth what God has said in heaven. If then the couple keeps speaking their vowels to God and to each other it will be to them according to their confession of the word of God.

The horizontal part of the ceremony is when the couple comes up and makes the same promise to each other. He says, "I take you to be my wife, to have and to hold from this day forward." She says the same, "To have and to hold, from this day forward." At its most basic, this is about the Eros in marriage. They are saying to each other, 'I commit my body only to you, I give my body only to you till one of us is dead.' And that was God's plan from the beginning. The Bible is plain about the role of Eros love in marriage. So, here's the big thought or idea, and most of what we are going to explore flows out of it. The big idea is: This is not my body. I don't own me, and you don't own you. Now that's about as counter-cultural as it gets. You hear it out there all the time. "This is my body; you can't tell me what to do with my body." Well, we are Jesus followers. Jesus followers understand that this is not my body. I don't own me, and you don't own you. God does own us, to begin with. Now I know that's not cool, but it's what we believe. Please read with me the following verses from our Bible. Psalm 24.1 "The earth is the Lord's, and everything in it. The world and all its people belong to him." We are part of that "everything," and we are one of those all its people.

GOD'S ORDER AND PURPOSE OF MARRIAGE

Which means, I don't own me, and you don't own you. We are his first. Paul addressing Jesus' followers said in 1 Corinthians 6:19 "Do you not know that your body is the temple of the Holy Spirit *who is* in you, whom you have from God, and you are not your own?"

I don't own me, and you don't own you. God has first claim. But for those of us who are married, it gets more complicated. The Bible says, "The wife does not have authority over her own body (really?!) but (she) yields (authority over her body) it to her husband (now that doesn't sound right!). In the same way, the husband does not have authority over his own body (really) but (he) yields (authority over his body) it to his wife." Well at least it is reciprocal. So, this body doesn't just belong to God, it's Eve's too. Eve's body doesn't just belong to God although it is his first, and because she is his first, she must be treated with respect. On their wedding day, Eve yielded authority over her body to Adam too. There is so much for, "It's my body; you can't tell me what to do with it!" This is God's truth. Well this truth that I don't belong to me and you don't belong to you has some profound implications for marriage. First it means that in a God-honoring marriage, sex is more about giving than getting. In fact, that's exactly what the Bible says. All things considered, therefore, don't hold yourselves back from sex unless you both agree to refrain from sexual intimacy for a limited time. This is not a reason to permit anybody to abuse you in the name of "The wife does not have authority over her own body but (she) yields (authority over her body) it to her husband" The wife is a good steward of God's body and makes sure it is not miss handled, misused and abused. It's her body yes, and she cannot do whatever she wants with it either. She can deprive her partner whenever she discerns she is being taken for a ride. But if it's her body too, and if marriage is more about giving than getting, then it's my responsibility to take care of my body and my partner sexually, and it's your responsibility to take care of your body and your partner sexually. There must be a balance. In a God-honoring marriage, you cannot withhold yourself – unless you both agree, for a limited time. Therefore: Now, historically, and culturally, there are several different perspectives on sex that just clash. First, A lot of people out there look at sex as just one of our natural appetites. We have a natural appetite for food, we have a natural appetite for sleep, we have a natural appetite for sex. When you're hungry, you eat; when you're tired, you sleep; when you are lusty, you take care of it, it's natural. And just like it's natural to sample different foods, it's natural to enjoy different sexual experiences. In fact, if sex is a natural appetite, and you repress it, it's unhealthy, right? By the way, that's a pretty common perspective out there.

Second Some people have a far more negative view of sex. They see sex as a necessary evil. You see there are two parts to every one of us. There is a physical part, our lower nature or fallen state and there is the rational part, the spiritual part, our higher nature. Sex is part of our lower nature. So, it feels degrading, it feels dirty. We do it, but we don't talk about it. Unfortunately, a whole lot of Jesus' followers usually go this way. They treat sex like it is a necessary evil. It is not evil neither is it the ultimate thing to do or route to go. Unfortunately, those who take the lower nature route are of the lower class and fail to treat this gift of God as treasure, but trash.

Chapter 27

Responsible Sexual Intimacy

The million-dollar question!

The million-dollar question is: What would you do if you lived in the medieval period and you are of the lower nature and have not crucified the **flesh** with its affections and **lust**s?

Sex in the medieval period sexual intercourse follow the teachings of the church, you would be forbidden to have sex 40 days before Christmas, 40 days before and 8 days after Easter, 8 days after Pentecost, on the eves of feast days, on Sundays to commemorate the resurrection, on Wednesday's to remember Lent, on Fridays to celebrate the crucifixion, during pregnancy, 30 days after birth, 40 days if the child is female, during menstruation, and 5 days before communion. That adds up to 252 excluded days, not counting feast days. They estimate about 30 days of those, meaning there were 83 days remaining days when husband and wife could have sex, provided of course the wife was not on her period, pregnant, or in the postnatal period, and providing they always intended to conceive a child. Therefore, the church advocated healthy sexuality!

The third perspective on sex out there is that sex is a form of self-expression. It is the way to find oneself to be when they live in the lower class, the lower nature. To the lower class it is a way to explore who one is and what they like. The lower nature thinks and speaks in a certain way. They say that if they want to reserve sex for marriage, that is cool too, that is their choice. If they want to pursue it outside of marriage, that is cool, that is their choice. If they want to experiment with various kinds of sexuality, if they want to be Eve, not Adam that is cool, that is their choice. If they want to explore porn, if they want to move from conquest to conquest in sexual sin, it is the way for them to be them, irrespective of what it does to others.

Now we who have been given power to become sons of God our perspective on sex must be God's perspective on sex. We are to live God's way, do life God's way and agree with him. Because God owns us. The fourth perspective is that, Now, sex is an appetite, planted in us by God and that's true. But here is the thing about appetites:

Animals are controlled by their appetites, we are not. We are different. We bear God's image. We can choose when and where and how to feed our appetites. And sometimes our choices are just bad. All of us get hungry, but some of us choose to eat too much, and we choose to eat the wrong stuff. You want proof? All of us get sleepy, but some of us choose to sleep too little, and some of us choose to sleep too much. You see, God gave us the freedom to choose how to feed our appetites and they don't control us. And all of us have a God-given desire for sex. But all of us can choose when, and where, and how. The choices we make don't just affect our bodies, but our hearts, souls, spirits, and the people we love.

A fifth perspective is that our hearts get all twisted up whenever we pursue sex outside the boundaries of marriage, where God intended it and the people we love always get hurt.

The sixth perspective is the idea that sex is a necessary evil, part of our lower nature? Well, that's just crazy. We don't believe the body is evil; we don't believe our God-given appetites are evil. Christianity is the most body-positive credo in the world? God created our physical world and he called it good – and we agree with him. He created our physical bodies, and he called them good – and we agree with him. God himself took a body in Jesus. And when Jesus comes back, we believe he's going to give us brand-new bodies – and it will be very good.

Seventh perspective is that all through the Bible God's people understood that sex was a gift, a magnificent gift from our God. It was God's idea, it was God's gift. The book of Song of Solomon poetry celebrates sex so openly. Any Jesus follower who thinks sex is bad or dirty needs to read the Bible. It's not a book for prudes or moralist. The idea that sex is a form of self-expression, a way to find myself and be myself, so there really are no rules and if you get hurt along the way, well, I've got to be me, and I have a right to be happy. Right! That's so pathetic! And here's the paradox: you won't discover yourself by living for yourself. You'll only discover who you really are -- who God meant you to be -- by living for others and living for God. The self-absorbed life is a petty one – it's far too little, it's unworthy. You will discover that a life loving God and loving others, a life that focuses on giving not getting is the kind of life that satisfies. That is where you will discover who you really are. Let us dig down and see what God wanted for us when he invented sex. What is it supposed to do for us, besides make babies, and to be honest, be great fun? Now the first-time sex is mentioned in the Bible is in Genesis 2.24. And through this sex, through this uniting, they virtually become one brand new person. The two become one: not just physically, but legally, socially, economically. Sex is part of what binds two people together into one brand new unit. And here's the deal: sex is both the sign of that union, and the means to accomplish it. Sex makes two one; and sex is a sign that two are one.

The eighth perspective on sex is more than just physically. You see, God never intended for us to unite with anyone physically unless we are willing to unite with them emotionally, socially, economically, and legally. God never intended for us to get naked with anyone unless we are willing to get naked with them in every other way. Once God joins us to someone in marriage, sex is one of God's ways that we maintain that union year after year till death do us part. That was God's plan. Sex is a covenant renewal ceremony. In marriage we do not just make a promise, we make a covenant. In fact, the Bible calls our spouse our "covenant friend." And all through the Bible there are these covenant renewal ceremonies. They would have these ceremonies to remind themselves who they were and what they stood for so as to renew the covenant. Sex is the most powerful way any of us can give ourselves to the other person. It's the way God designed for two people to say to each other, "I belong to you. I belong to you completely, permanently, and exclusively." Everything sex means in marriage is cheapened when a person has sex outside of marriage. It becomes so much less than what God made it to be. It degrades the covenant we make with our spouse. Paul was not anti-sex, but anti anything that would cheapen sex. One thing he tells us is that a Jesus follower can't have sex with a prostitute. And it's not because of the STDs, or because he is a prude or moralist. He says, "Don't you realize that if a man joins himself to a prostitute, he becomes one body with her? For the Scriptures say in Genesis 2:24, 'The two are united into one'". It is always more than "just sex." It's the uniting of two into one.

My ninth perspective on sex is that we must not pursue the kind of sex that avoids commitment and intimacy, leaving us lonelier than ever. This kind of sex that sex that avoids commitment and intimacy can never 'become one.' That would cheapen it. And it would degrade covenant love, the only kind of love that lasts. So, Paul says, "It's stupid, it is dishonest, to give your body to someone to whom you don't intend to give your whole life." A lot of people think this view of sex is too narrow. They argue "It's just sex," right? They figure that the idea of waiting till marriage is stupid and unrealistic. They think that the idea of waiting till marriage is unhealthy. They think that even in marriage a little bit of fooling around is perfectly fine, maybe even healthy and yet, their experience, and your experience proves what Paul is trying to tell us. If God designed sex to unite two persons into one, then it shouldn't surprise anybody that people feel that incredible sense of union even when they use sex wrong. You've seen it happen. You've seen it happen on TV; you've seen it happen to your friends; you may have even felt it in your own life. Two people have sex outside of marriage, and immediately they start saying things like, "I'll always love you." "I want to spend the rest of my life with you." "I'll never let you go." And even though they are not married, they start to feel connected. So, when he doesn't call her back the next day, she gets hurt. Because sex was designed by God to create a covenant, and to renew that covenant. So, when he wants to break it off, she gets intensely jealous, and even obsessive, she gets hurt. Think Fatal Attraction, or Play Misty for Me. And so, does the real wife, or the real husband, and the kids – because "the cheater was supposed to be in covenant with me, we gave ourselves to each other in every way." And if the sex happens before marriage, the power of sex to make two into one causes a whole lot of people to get trapped in a marriage that is not healthy, because their emotions are drown out their brains. Once they start having sex, they go brain dead. I have done quite a bit of pre-marital counseling and here is one thing I have seen, a lot. I will see two people who are just mismatched. I mean a terrible match. Sometimes I wonder what's pushing them. I have found out a lot of times, it's because they have already started the sex. Sex has such power to make two one.

Tenth view on sex is that it overrides acquaintances' brains, and plants this deep sense of obligation. That's how God designed sex and that's why he tells us to reserve it for marriage. It creates covenant, and it renews covenant. And when people have sex outside their marriage, it erodes the covenant they have made with their spouse, at the same time it is softening your heart towards another. Sex creates covenant, and it renews covenant which is why God designed it for marriage. It is too powerful for us in any other context.

Two kinds of people will be reading this book. Those unmarried and the married. First, those of you who are struggling to wait till marriage I need to say some things to you. It can be hard especially when you are carnal and not spiritual because sex is one of God's most powerful gifts. It is a powerful God-given appetite, but one must exercise self-control.

First, develop some fierce convictions. Get clear about what God wants. That can be hard when we disregard God's designed purpose for sex and start rationalizing and compromising. God created sex for marriage to reflect His image. If you don't understand why, you must trust Him. He is smarter than we are. And He is not making life hard, but great. If you don't agree with God on waiting till marriage, wait anyway. He is God and you are not. He owns you and you don't.

The Bible says, "Run from sexual sin." *1Corinthians 6:18 - Flee sexual immorality. Every sin that a man does is outside the body, but he who commits sexual immorality sins against his own body.* Run away, don't walk, run! In fact, sexual sin is the only sin the Bible tells us to run from. It is so powerful, seductive, and has such power to spoil what God wants for you. If you are tempted to sin every time you are in his room alone together, don't be in his room alone together. It is not smart to put yourself in a place where you know you are going to struggle. Don't put yourself in a place where you are going to struggle and then ask God to give you the strength to resist sin. That is stupid. Run from sexual sin.

Third, if you stumble and fall, don't be crippled by your failures. Having sex before marriage or outside of marriage is not the unpardonable sin. Don't let your guilt and your shame drive you away from the grace of God. God doesn't take sin lightly. Jesus died for it. But neither does God want us to wallow in our shame and guilt. Accept His grace. If you don't, you are just going to make it harder the next time you are tempted.

To the married, first remember, you don't own yourself. God owns you first; and you gave yourself to your husband or your wife when the Lord joins you to marriage.

1 Corinthians 7:4 The wife does not have authority over her own body, but the husband does. Likewise, the husband does not have authority over his own body, but the wife does.

GOD'S ORDER AND PURPOSE OF MARRIAGE

Second , Because of that, we don't withhold sex from each other, in **God joint marriage**. It's not just about me; what I want, what I need. Remember what it goes on to say? *1 Corinthians 7:5 "All things considered abstaining from sex is permissible for a period if you both agree to it ... but only for a fleeting time. Then come back together."*

Third, for how long? for how many years do we pursue sex in our marriages? When you are in covenant, covenant renewal is appropriate. If you have the ability, and if your partner has the desire, we serve each other, we renew our covenant until death do us part. The bond between a husband and wife is a lifetime commitment. 1 Corinthians 7:39 - *A wife is bound by law as long as her husband lives; but if her husband dies, she is at liberty to be married to whom she wishes, only in the Lord.* A wife is bound to her husband during all the time her husband is alive. Please understand that death does not only refer to cessation of life, but it also refers to death in abandoning marriage roles. Marriage covenant is enforced by working out marriage roles. Husbands who purposely fail to love, provide, protect, lead their wives

Fourth, sex will change. We are different as we grow older and our bodies are different. Time, children, ailments, age all force changes to our sexual intimacy. But if you have the ability, and if your partner has the desire, you will figure something out till death do you part.

One of the reasons there are so many ineffective Christians is because most don't have a one on one personal intimate relationship with God and spouses. It is not only those in ministry that are to be in relationship with God and spouses. We are all to know Him and be in relationship with Him and our marriage relationship will be strong. How can you love someone with all your heart, mind, soul, and strength if you don't know them? You must know and love your spouse the way God stipulates in His word.

Chapter 28

SEX-casual Marriage

Ephesians 5:3 declares, "But among you there must not be even a hint of sexual immorality, or of any kind of impurity...because these are improper for God's holy people." 1 Corinthians 7:2 gives us the biblical definition of "immorality" as any form of sexual contact outside of marriage. According to Hebrews 13:4, only the "marriage bed" is pure and undefiled.

Therefore, according to the Bible, sex is to be reserved for marriage, Period. So, oral sex is a sin if done before or outside of marriage.

When Is oral sex a sin if done within a marriage? Many, perhaps most, Christian married couples have had this question. *1* Corinthians 7:5 declares "Do not deprive one another except with consent for a time, that you may give yourselves to fasting and prayer; and come together again so that Satan does not tempt you because of your lack of self-control." All things considered, the principle of "mutual consent" applies. Although this text specifically deals with abstaining from sex and frequency of sex, "mutual consent" is a concept that applies universally in regard to sex within marriage. Whatever is done, it should be fully agreed on between the husband and his wife. Neither spouse should be forced or coerced into doing something he or she is not completely comfortable with. If oral sex is done within the confines of marriage and in the spirit of mutual consent, there is not a biblical case for declaring it to be a sin.

It is important for husband and wife to make sure that the two of them have a SEX-cessful marriage. A number of you may grimace, smirk and be horrified, however this is part of what spices marriage.

But truth be known, 1 Corinthians 7:1-5 explains it all. These verses answer several questions: What is God's answer to my sex drive? How do I handle my struggles with self-control? When sexual temptations arise, how can I defeat them? All these questions and more are answered in *1 Corinthians 7:1-5 "Now concerning the things of which you wrote to me:*

It is good for a man not to touch a woman. ² Nevertheless, because of sexual immorality, let each man have his own wife, and let each woman have her own husband. ³ Let the husband render to his wife the affection due her, and likewise also the wife to her husband. ⁴ The wife does not have authority over her own body, but the husband does. And likewise, the husband does not have authority over his own body, but the wife does. ⁵ Do not deprive one another except with consent for a time, that you may give yourselves to fasting and prayer; and come together again so that Satan does not tempt you because of your lack of self-control." Sex should not be looked upon as a duty. It means be faithful to each other. It DOES NOT give the man the right to demand sex whenever he wants. Nor does it take away the right of the woman to refuse sex with her husband. In fact, it doesn't impart any rights at all. Dishonorable spouses offend their spouses which erodes all the affection and there is nothing left to give. In a nutshell, God commands us to *satisfy and protect our spouse.*

We are exhorted to fulfill our sexual desires through a loving, sacrificial relationship with our spouse. The words, "Now concerning" prepares us for God's response to the questions What is God's answer to my sex drive? How do I handle my struggles with self-control? When sexual temptations arise, how can I defeat them?

The phrase, "it is good for a man not to touch a woman," has nothing to do with a hug, a handshake, or any other manifestation of fellowship or friendship. To "touch a woman" is an inoffensive word for sexual intercourse. The mindset of the Corinthians went way beyond issues of marriage or even celibacy. The natural question is, "Why would the Corinthians not be interested in sexual intercourse in the context of marriage?" There were some in the congregation who believed that the highest plane of spirituality is to forgo sex. They prioritized the spirit over the body and there are those who justified sexual immorality because what they did in the body was as important as what they did in the spirit. Those who esteem the soul can argue that it is best for one to deny as many physical needs as possible. Obviously, both of these extremes are unbiblical.

1 Corinthians 7:3 *"The husband must fulfill his duty to his wife, and likewise also the wife to her husband."* is an exhortation and clarification explaining each spouse's sexual responsibilities in marriage. This verse means what every man hopes it means! To many this is one of the greatest verses in the Bible. It is a duty that they delight in. It is the one job they want to spend overtime at. But before you get too carried away, notice a number of things:

First, it begins by addressing husbands. It says, it is the husband's duty to fulfill his wife. Now many of you husbands are saying, "Now this is one Bible verse I'll be glad to take literally." Hold your peace! It begins with husbands because they are the ones that are ultimately responsible for the sexual relationship. They are the spiritual leaders! Husband, here the scripture indicates that you must "fulfill" your wife. **This doesn't just mean sex. It means finding out what she needs, when she needs it, and how she needs it. I realize that you don't have an idea how to do this.** That's where communication kicks in. You are responsible for facilitating communication with your wife. Ladies, this means that you have to tell your husband how he can "minister" to you. If you do not communicate and respond to him well, he will become disillusioned and frustrated. If he ignores your communication, you are not in bondage and obligated to do anything.

Second, it begins with husbands because they often neglect to fulfill this command. In the course of my ministry, I have known many men who have struggled to fulfill their duty than women. A big misnomer is that wives are the ones that always have a headache. This is not always true. Some husbands are too tired when it is time for sexual intercourse. Many men are addicted to porn, which takes away a husband's sexual drive for his wife. Others, it is just a matter of laziness. Some men know that sex can take a while and they are just lazy, so they fail to fulfill their duty to their wife. Yet, wives experience intimacy through sex. Furthermore, when you deprive your wife of sex, she is left feeling like you don't find her attractive. Husband, *satisfy and protect your wife*.

Third, honor and elevate women. Jesus always took a high view of women. To some uniformed the norm is that the husband dominates the wife. In Christian marriages, there is a mutuality of relationship. The scripture clearly elevates women and also declares them to be sexual creatures that have desires and needs. Husbands, this means you must meet the sexual needs of your wife. This includes her emotional, mental, and spiritual needs as well. When you put your wife's needs first, by God's grace, your sexual needs will be met as well.

Now, wives, this verse also applies to you. You are commanded by God to fulfill your husband's sexual needs who has not departed or abandoned his responsibilities. The word "fulfill," used her means "to make full, to bring to completion, to develop the full potential." The word fulfill is a present active command. This means that you should ensure that your husband who is alive in acts of intercession to you is fully satisfied and vice versa. Ladies, whatever your husband wants that is not immoral or illegal all things considered, give it to him. Make sure that your marriage bed is so hot that your husband will not ever go looking elsewhere! There is nothing dirty about this; it is entirely biblical. Why should the world have the greatest sex? The greatest sex should be among married couples who are devoted to Christ. Wife, *satisfy and protect your spouse who is alive in acts of intercession*.

Living husbands in acts of intercession and wives, please understand, this verse teaches that sex is a delight, but it is also a duty. A "duty" is a moral or legal responsibility or obligation that arises from one's position. It is the duty of each married person to meet the sexual needs of his or her partner. This means sex should never be used as a bribe or reward for good behavior, or as something to be withheld as a threat or punishment. It is a "duty!" The spouse who withholds sex sins against God and his or her partner.

For instance, let's say the husband who has not abandoned his roles in marriage makes sexual overtures to his wife. The Bible teaches that it is her responsibility as his wife to have sex. Why? Because in this case, the husband has a sexual drive, seeking fulfillment and it's her duty to make sure his needs are met. Therefore, whenever your spouse initiates sex in your direction, make sure you keep in mind that you are under God-given direction to meet your spouse's sexual needs. This is what you signed up for. You made this commitment before God and men. Therefore, before a couple gets married, the question needs to be asked, "Are you willing to be sexually available to your spouse till physical or roles death do you part?" If the answer is, "Well, I'm not so sure about that," I would suggest that the couple postpone their marriage or not get married at all.

Let's us pose a question: Which of the two marital partners must be the one to decide if the sexual drives or desires are completely satisfied? The one initiating sex. In other words, the only way a husband can know if he has "fulfilled his duty" as a husband is to ask his wife, "Are your sexual needs fully satisfied? Do you feel loved?" This means, in the bedroom of a married couple anything goes—short of illegal or immoral activity.

How often should sex occur? If the average couple has sex 2-3 times a week, should Christians who are filled with the Holy Spirit and called to live supernatural lives have sex more or less frequently? I'll give you my personal bias. The more frequent your sex, the stronger your marriage bond.

Why should married partners always fulfill their duty to their spouse? This is a legitimate question that is answered in 1 Corinthians 7:4. *"The wife does not have authority over her own body, but the husband does; and likewise, also the husband does not have authority over his own body, but the wife does."* God sovereignly takes something away at the point of marriage and gives it as a heavenly wedding present to your spouse. The Lord doesn't ask you if He can take it, and the Lord doesn't ask you if you want it. Sovereignly, the Lord takes the authority you have had over your own body as a single individual and removes it from you for as long as you live. The term "authority" in this passage literally means to have rights over or exclusive claim to. In simple terms, God gave my body to my wife and I have nothing to say about it.

Note that both husband and wife are given equal rights in these verses. The husband is not regarded as having sexual rights or needs that the wife does not have or vice versa. So, if your wife wants to feel your muscles, let her feel them. If your husband wants to grab your underpart, let him grab it. This principle applies in the sexual realm; however, I believe there is great application in other areas of life. Several examples come to mind: tattoos, piercings, facial hair, length of hair, attire, birth control, body appearance, etc. are all decisions that your husband or wife can veto. We ought to ask, "How can I look better to you? What do you want from me? How can I serve you?"

The term "body" is frequently used here in its broadest, fullest, richest sense. It's everything we are physically, emotionally, and spiritually. We are designed by God to be an instrument of communication verbally, nonverbally, emotionally, physically, and sexually. The physical expression of sexual intercourse as communication is enjoyed in the larger context of verbal communication. The greatest sexual fulfillment comes gradually over the long haul in a marriage, as a couple learns to speak about anything, any time; when there's heart-to-heart communication, not just talking at each other, but listening actively and sensitively, caring deeply about the communication. How are you doing in these areas today?

If God were to ask your spouse, what would he or she say? Would your spouse be fulfilled and pleased by how you are treating her body or his body?

1 Corinthians 7:5 closes with these potent words: *"Stop depriving one another, except by agreement for a time, so that you may devote yourselves to prayer, and come together again so that Satan will not tempt you because of your lack of self-control."* The word "stop depriving" literally means "do not rob one another," or "do not do fraud to one another." The word means to cheat somebody out of what is properly theirs. If you withhold your body when your partner seeks sex, it is biblical fraud. Have you failed to *satisfy and protect your spouse*? You may deprive each other of sex under various conditions.

First, Sexual Intimacy can be withheld when you both agree. You can't decide by yourself to deprive your spouse of sex. Both of you must agree not to have sex in order to fit into this exception. Here's how this may work in real life: Let's say that last night your spouse rolled over in bed and made a sexual advance. Because you had a long and exhausting day, you said, "I'm really tired tonight. Would it be alright with you if we waited until tomorrow night? If not, sweetheart, you know that tonight is okay too. What would you like?"

Biblically speaking, who has the final say in this decision? The initiating partner always has the final say. If your spouse wants sex, even after hearing your request, he or she still has authority over your body. However, just because your body belongs to your spouse doesn't mean you don't have the freedom to negotiate! When the initiating partner hears a willing but tired attitude of acceptance rather than rejection, understanding should be forthcoming.

Second, Sexual Intimacy can be deprived when you both agree to delay it for a time. The two must agree when they will have sexual intimacy. For a time here means a *specific period* of time. Whenever a couple mutually agrees to deprive one another of sexual intimacy, To agree only to "not tonight" would not be following the biblical pattern.

Third, Sexual Intimacy can be set aside to devote yourselves to prayer. This certainly presents a clear and rather unusual freedom for depriving yourself of sexual intimacy in modern society. The purpose for depriving yourselves of sex is to devote yourselves to sharing a spiritual focus in your marriage.

Fourth, Sexual Intimacy can be deprived until the two of you agree to come together again.

The scripture quickly brings us back to the reality that sexual intimacy is to be the norm and never the exception. Always remember, we are called to *satisfy and protect our spouse.*

Fifth, ***Sexual Intimacy can be deprived if the husband departs from his roles in the marriage.*** *Whenever a husband departs or abandons his roles of providing, protection and leadership in marriage scripturally he is considered as dead. He breaches the marriage covenant. The wife is widowed and at that point The Lord takes over and becomes her husband* Isaiah 54:5

Now, there are two important realities to keep in mind. ***First, if you deprive each other you open yourself to attack.*** Paul blatantly states that in sexual matters, you must come together after an agreed upon time of sexual abstinence, or you will open yourself up to satanic attack. After a period of time without sex, you are to come together again. If you don't, Satan will come against you with temptations to commit sexual immorality. The longer sex is postponed in the marital partnership, the greater the risk of temptation.

Please take this very seriously. Satan is not a pushover. He is real and powerful. He holds millions firmly in his bondage. And he is seeking more all the time. The Bible gives a true picture of what Satan is about in the world. And you would learn that, among other things, he is about the destruction of marriages. He is totally committed to adultery, and all the personal problems that lead to it. When you battle with sexual temptation, you battle against Satan. Not because he creates the desire, but because he so powerfully and deceptively uses the desire.

As married couples, we must guard our marriages from Satan. He is seeking to devour the marriage bed. Therefore, don't let him into your bed. Imagine this common scenario: A couple in bed with their back turned to each other and plenty of space in between. Guess who can slither right into the marriage bed? A simple way to avoid this is being close before you drift off to sleep. Roll over and cuddle your partner every night. Put your head on his or her chest or shoulder. Play "footsies." If these intimate moments lead to sexual intimacy… wonderful. But regardless, you have shared some intimate moments and are taking one additional step to protect the marriage bed.

Second, you lack self-control when you deprive each other of Sexual Intimacy. What happens to married individuals when they don't have sexual intimacy for a period of days? Satan tempts you, taking advantage of your lack of self-control. Depriving your spouse of sexual relations results in more than immediate, short-lived frustration. Continued postponement of sexual relations within a marriage places very real and unnecessary pressure on a spouse.

Sexual response and impulse touches us more than physically, it also touches us emotionally and spiritually because God made us that way. We have to avoid two opposite evils. On the one hand, the believe that the highest plane of spirituality is to forgo sex that wants to deny sex, calling it something dirty, and lock it away; and on the other hand, the more modern hedonism that tells us sex is an absolute good and that we ought to pursue our sexual impulses no matter what.

If we Christians ignore sex, we will surrender it to those very cultural perversions and give the impression that sex itself is bad *because* it is so abused. But you cannot fix what is wrong by simply negating or ignoring it. Nobody lives in the world of "no." We all have to know how to say "Yes" in the right way. It's not enough to be people who hate evil; we must also be people who love good, and we must teach our children to love good. We are negatively labelled and known as "people who say 'No' to everything." We are much better at saying what not to do than what to do. Sexuality is deeply perverted in our culture. But we have to do more than negate the negative. We also have to articulate powerfully the joy of God's way, to show the beauty of holiness. The word of the Lord for us today is to *satisfy and protect our spouse.*

Chapter 29

Signs of DOOMED Relationship

There are obvious warning signs to watch out for and discover that your marriage relationship is over with. It will take serious measures which is working out one's Soul's salvation to redeem it.

Marriage relationships can be problematic, and no one wants to feel like they are wasting time. However, it's not always easy to tell if your relationship is going well or if it's over and dying a slow death. There are the usual telltale signs your relationship is over like lots of fighting and distrust, but there can also be less obvious signs that you don't want to miss if you want to stay in love.

There are a few things that you should be paying attention to in order to figure out how your relationship is going.

1. Your partner disrespects you.

One immediate sign is if a partner belittles the other and treats them with disrespect, privately or publicly.

2. Your partner emotionally abuses you.

Another sign of emotional abuse can be a partner who is very charming and nice in public but who changes completely once the front door is closed. One of the first signs of domestic abuse is someone not wanting their partner to see friends and family or to work outside the home. This kind of behavior tends to come on gradually and is a sign of a controlling partner.

3. You perceive incompatibility.

There are other warning signs, like not being able to think of things to talk about, or not wanting much physical contact; however, these things aren't necessarily signs your relationship is dying and heading for rough waters. Sometimes people just need assistance with learning how to properly communicate , and other times, a person's childhood or upbringing can make them less inclined to touch. But if neither has anything to say to the other, yes, that feels like an incompatible relationship.

4. You act on your fantasies of having a different life.

Even if you find yourself wondering what life would be like if you left your partner, it doesn't mean that the relationship is doomed. However, it is healthy to daydream about different life scenarios, although acting on them is not a great idea in all cases. We all imagine different futures, and this can be a good way of reminding yourself about what you value about your current set up. The question is, can you achieve what you want to achieve in life and stay in this relationship?

5. You have the same fight over and over again.

When you find yourself always fighting the same battles with your partner, it may mean that one of you has some deeper issue that needs to be worked out. If you find yourself having the same argument all the time, that is a sign that you would benefit from spiritual help. There is usually an unconscious element in why we choose our partners, sometimes the reasons are not so healthy and so it is important to become more aware of why we might be repeating the same patterns.

Chapter 30

Remarriage

A spouse is eligible for remarriage after being widowed. In 1 Corinthians 7:8-9 and 1 Timothy 5:14 the Bible speaks about remarriage after a spouse dies, it actually encourages it. 1 Corinthians 7:8-9 [8] But I say to the unmarried and to the widows: It is good for them if they remain even as I am; [9] but if they cannot exercise self-control, let them marry. For it is better to marry than to burn with passion.

1 Timothy 5:14 Therefore I desire that the younger widows marry, bear children, manage the house, give no opportunity to the adversary to speak reproachfully.

The Jewish culture in biblical times also encouraged remarriage for several reasons. It is interesting to note that the Bible addresses the issue of widows rather than widowers. However, there is nothing within the context of any of these passages leading us to believe that the standard was gender-specific.

Addressing widows primarily had most likely to be for several reasons.

First, men usually worked outside the home, sometimes doing dangerous jobs. Men today just as in biblical times, have shorter life spans on average than their wives. Thus, widows were far more common than widowers.

The second, is the fact that women rarely had any means of supporting themselves and their children in biblical times. *2 Kings 4:1-7 - A certain woman of the wives of the sons of the prophets cried out to Elisha, saying, "Your servant my husband is dead, and you know that your servant feared the LORD. And the creditor is coming to take my two sons to be his slaves."*

² So Elisha said to her, "What shall I do for you? Tell me, what do you have in the house?" And she said, "Your maidservant has nothing in the house but a jar of oil."

³ Then he said, "Go, borrow vessels from everywhere, from all your neighbors—empty vessels; do not gather just a few. ⁴ And when you have come in, you shall shut the door behind you and your sons; then pour it into all those vessels, and set aside the full ones."⁵ So she went from him and shut the door behind her and her sons, who brought the vessels to her; and she poured it out. ⁶ Now it came to pass, when the vessels were full, that she said to her son, "Bring me another vessel." And he said to her, "There is not another vessel." So, the oil ceased. ⁷ Then she came and told the man of God. And he said, "Go, sell the oil and pay your debt; and you and your sons live on the rest."

Remarriage was the primary way in which a widow would regain protection and provision for the needs of herself and her children. Once Christ established the Church, the Church became responsible for the care of widows under certain circumstances 1 Timothy 5:3-10 Honor widows who are really widows. ⁴ But if any widow has children or grandchildren, let them first learn to show piety at home and to repay their parents; for this is good and acceptable before God. ⁵ Now she who is really a widow, and left alone, trusts in God and continues in supplications and prayers night and day. ⁶ But she who lives in [b]pleasure is dead while she lives. ⁷ And these things command, that they may be blameless. ⁸ But if anyone does not provide for his own, and especially for those of his household, he has denied the faith and is worse than an unbeliever.

⁹Do not let a widow under sixty years old be taken into the number, and not unless she has been the wife of one man, ¹⁰ well reported for good works: if she has brought up children, if she has lodged strangers, if she has washed the saints' feet, if she has relieved the afflicted, if she has diligently followed every excellent work.

The third issue was that continuing the husband's family line because name was a concern in Jewish culture. Therefore, if a husband died without leaving any children to carry on his name, his brother was encouraged to marry the widow and provide her with children. Other men in the family had the option also, but there was a proper order in which each man had the opportunity to fulfill or pass on this responsibility. The example of this is in the book of Ruth. Even among priests who had to follow a higher standard, remarriage after the death of a spouse was permitted. In the case of priests, it was under the stipulation that they only marry the widow of another priest *Ezekiel 44:15, 22* – ¹⁵But the priests, the Levites, the sons of Zadok, who kept charge of My sanctuary when the children of Israel went astray from Me, they shall come near Me to minister to Me; and they shall stand before Me to offer to Me the fat and the blood," says the Lord GOD. They shall not take as wife a widow or a divorced woman but take virgins of the descendants of the house of Israel, or widows of priests. However, this is not a cultural, traditional, or religious matter. **1 Corinthians 6:12** Paul says that - *The Body Is the Lord's.* Everything is **permissible** for me, but not all things are beneficial. Everything is **permissible** for me, but I will not be enslaved by anything and brought under its power, allowing it to control me.

1 Corinthians 10:23 - All things are lawful that is, morally legitimate, **permissible**, but not all things are beneficial *or* advantageous. All things are lawful, but not all things are constructive to character *and* edifying to spiritual life.

Therefore, based on all biblical instruction on the subject, remarriage after the death of a spouse is permitted by God, but not according to the culture and men's traditions or religious dogma.

When a male man and female man get married, God unites them as one flesh Genesis 2:24 Therefore a man shall leave his father and mother and be joined to his wife, and they shall become one flesh. Matthew 19:4-6 And He answered and said to them, "Have you not read that He who made *them* at the beginning 'made them male and female,'⁵ and said, 'For this reason a man shall leave his father and mother and be joined to his wife, and the two shall become one flesh'? ⁶So then, they are no longer two but one flesh. Therefore, what God has joined together, let not man separate.

The only thing that can break the marriage bond for those God has joint, in his eyes, is death both physical and spiritual. If a person's spouse dies, the widow / widower is absolutely free to remarry. The Apostle Paul allowed widows to remarry in and encouraged younger widows to remarry. Remarriage after the death of a spouse is absolutely allowed by God.

Widowed spouses get totally devastated by their loss. They get so tired of feeling lost and lonely. Though they may have no desire to remarry, they would like at least to have some companionship with the opposite gender. But these thoughts make them feel so guilty and disloyal to their late spouses, who are now with the Lord. Now the question is what should they do?

You sense loneliness because you have been severed from a living part of yourself and lost because you don't know what to do next. You are unable to envision how the rest of your life is supposed to go, now that the life you shared with your late spouse has been taken away. What next? This is one of the huge questions "Who am I?" meaning-of-life moments that we don't expect to have again after we marry and settle down. Once we have begun a successful relationship, it takes on its own existence. When this union is broken the surviving partner feels disoriented, feeling like an amputee.

The surrounding community has the responsibility to offer the bereaved a role that is useful, honorable, and fulfilling. The surviving spouse is not a beneficiary. Few single people in our culture do, because pairing up is relentlessly presented as the only choice. Singles are continually pushed together and prompted to find a mate, as if anything short of couple-life is deficient.

Christians desperately need to recover a way of seeing the single life as valid on its own terms, and not simply as a holding tank. Though never-marrieds are made to feel like failures, that would hardly be history's judgment of their notable example, the apostle Paul. He found his life so fulfilling that he said, "I wish that all were as I myself am. "1 Corinthians 7:7 - For I wish that all men were even as I myself. But each one has his own gift from God, one in this manner and another in that. **⁸** But I say to the unmarried and to the widows: It is good for them if they remain even as I am."

Divorce for spousal abandonment or desertion

1 Corinthians 7:10-16 - Many Christians mistakenly think this is just talking about relationships between a believing and non-believing spouses. But the principle of a spouse departing remains the same whether that spouse is a believer or not.

Spousal abandonment or desertion does not refer to literal departure only. It includes departure or abandonment of spousal roles or responsibilities which could be a reason enough to divorce that God would honor. Let me explain. God will not allow any of His children to be in bondage in any setting. Christians spouses are God's children and He will defend them. The angels of protection, provision, love, peace, prosperity, wealth and blessing will avenge them. I know that for sure. I also know that sounds very liberal and not religious and traditional as we have been taught. You see this is part of the problem and bondage. Religion and traditions of men make the word of God of no effect and are binding by themselves. Spouses are God's children and they must be set free to serve **in** their Lord's vineyard.

GOD'S ORDER AND PURPOSE OF MARRIAGE

Roles of the husband and wife in a marriage setting are diverse and have adverse lasting effects both positive and negative.

Males and females are equal in relationship to Christ. The Scriptures give specific roles to each in marriage. According to 1 Corinthians 11:3 and Ephesians 5:23, the husband is to assume leadership in the home. This leadership should not be dictatorial, condescending, or patronizing to the wife, but should be in accordance with the example of Christ leading the church. Ephesians 5:25-26 States, "Husbands, love your wives, just as Christ loved the church and gave himself up for her to make her holy, cleansing her by the washing with water through the word." Christ loved the church, His people with compassion, mercy, forgiveness, respect, and selflessness. In this same way husbands are to love their wives.

Wives are to submit to the authority of their husbands as to the Lord. That means as is fitting in the Lord. "Wives, submit to your husbands as to the Lord. For the husband is the head of the wife as Christ is the head of the church, his body, of which he is the Savior. Now as the church submits to Christ, so also wives should submit to their husbands in everything in the Lord." Ephesians 5:22-24. **Wives should never allow themselves to be put under bondage, oppression, suppression, devoured or abused in the name of submission**. The Bible tells husbands severally how they are supposed to treat their wives. The husband is not to take on the role of the dictator but should show respect for his wife and her opinions. In fact, Ephesians 5:28-29 exhorts men to love their wives in the same way that they love their own bodies, feeding and caring for them. A husband's love for his wife should be the same as Christ's love for His body, the church.

"Wives, submit to your husbands, as is fitting in the Lord. Husbands, love your wives and do not be harsh with them" Colossians 3:18-19. "Husbands, in the same way be considerate as you live with your wives, and treat them with respect as the weaker partner and as heirs with you of the gracious gift of life, so that nothing will hinder your prayers" 1 Peter 3:7. From these verses we see that love and respect characterize the roles of both husbands and wives. If these are present, then authority, headship, love, and submission will not be a problem for either partner.

The Bible instructs husbands' part of their responsibilities in the home is to provide for their families. He is to work and make enough money to sufficiently provide all the necessities of life for his wife to manage the home. Failure to doing so has definite spiritual consequences. 1 Timothy 5:8 declares "If anyone does not provide for his relatives, and especially for his immediate family, he has denied the faith and is worse than an unbeliever. That means a man who makes no effort to provide for his family cannot rightly call himself a Christian. The wife is a helper in supporting the family, but not the provider.

Proverbs 31:10, 13-15 – "Who can find a virtuous wife? For her worth *is* far above rubies. [13] She willingly works with her hands. [14] She is like the merchant ships, She brings her food from afar. [15] She also rises while it is yet night, and provides food for her household, And a portion for her maidservants."

That does not give a husband an excuse of relinquishing, abandoning, or departing from his role and responsibility of providing in the family. A godly wife may surely help but providing for the family is not primarily her responsibility, it is her husband's. While a husband should help with the children and with household chores thereby fulfilling his duty to love his wife it is evident that the home is to be the wife's primary area of influence, management, responsibility, and not to do the house work. The wife is not a slave, house worker, or a servant, but she is simply a manager of the home. The husband is to provide help and labor by hiring house help to the wife and the she will manage the home proficiently. Even if she must stay up late and rise up early, her family is well cared for. Nowadays, this is not an easy lifestyle for many wives experiencing affluence of freedom and liberation especially in developing nations. Far too many wives from primitive oppressive cultures of traditions and religion are stressed out and stretched to the breaking point. To prevent such stress, both husband and wife should prayerfully reorder their priorities and follow the Bible's instructions on their roles.

Conflicts of division of roles in a marriage may occur, but if both partners are submitted to Christ, these conflicts will be minimal. If a couple finds arguments over this issue are frequent and vehement, or if arguments seem to characterize the marriage, the problem is a spiritual one. In such an instance, the partners should recommit themselves to prayer and submission to Christ first, then to each other in an attitude of love and respect.

Christ's word on divorce is that God does not want husbands and wives divorcing each other without a cause that God approves of. But God will allow divorce for the sin of abandonment, departure and relinquishing of roles and responsibilities in marriage. **In I Corinthians 7:15 "But if the unbelieving departs, let him depart. A brother or a sister is not under bondage in such cases but God has called us to peace."** Paul does not say divorce – he says "not under bondage

Some Christians will say "Paul does not use the word divorce, but he simply says they are not under bondage" – meaning the person cannot divorce and remarry. The word "divorce" does not have to be used.

In Exodus 21:10-11 says that - "^{10} If he takes another *wife*, he shall not diminish her food, her clothing, and her marriage rights. ^{11} And if he does not do these three for her, then she shall go out free, without *paying* money."

Divorce is spoken of as a wife being "free". In the same way when Paul says a "brother or sister is not under bondage in such cases" – he is saying they are freed from that marriage. This cause for divorce applies equally to both genders. **"A brother or a sister** is not under bondage in such cases." It is clear that both a husband and a wife can divorce their spouse for abandonment. This is not a gender specific cause for divorce.

How long must one wait in cases of abandonment before they can remarry? The Bible does not specify a wait time in cases of abandonment. God does not require a believer to be bound to a spouse that abandons them. Marriage requires two people, if one departs then the marriage covenant has been breached and there is no more marriage.

Chapter 31

What a Wife Looks for in Marriage

There are four most basic needs a wife longs for in Marriage and **we will not have done our duty if we don't state that a wife's most basic needs in marriage are to be loved, cherished, known, and respected.**

Cherish Your Wife

Your Wife Needs to be Cherished. Husbands need to realize that their love-starved wives would trade everything in the world for a little tenderness from them. Without meaning to, a husband can completely miss one of his wife's most important needs, to be cherished. This need is too often overlooked by husbands because we don't feel the need for it as deeply as wives do. But that doesn't discount its validity. Your wife needs to be cherished. She needs to know she is number one in your life. If it came down to an evening with your buddies or a night with your wife, she needs to know you would choose her not because you have to, but because you want to hold her dear, show her affection as the only friend you will ever have. There are some things you can do to cherish your wife. First Consider how often you say, "I love you" and second whether you make her feel important.

It is heartening to always tell your wife "I love you." Some husbands don't feel the need to say "I love you every time, but every wife has an insatiable need to hear it. Your wife also needs evidence that you are thinking about her during your day. A small gift or a quick phone call to say, "You are on my mind," can mean the world to her. As a husband, you probably have no idea of the effect you can have on your wife by being gentle and tender, making her feel cared for.

Cherishing your wife does not mean sacrificing everything. When your wife is satisfied in knowing that she takes first place in your life, when she knows she is the most important thing in the world to you, she will encourage you to do the things you enjoy. It is part of the mystery of marriage. When a wife is truly, genuinely cherished, she feels free to encourage her husband's independence.

It is a win-win situation to always make your wife feel important. Before a husband learns to cherish his wife, she will complain about everything. In fact, she would like a separation because you consider taking care of everything else is more important to you than she is. But once a husband genuinely makes his wife number one, once he begins to express true tenderness, your wife will pleasantly shock you. She will encourage you to do what you want. She will make this offer because she now feels secure in her position of importance. "To love and to cherish" is more than a phrase from your wedding vows. It is one of the most important needs your wife will ever have. By meeting it, you are sure to build a partnership that brings to both of you pleasure.

Your Wife Needs to be Known. To a wife, being understood means having her feelings validated and accepted. That is not as easy as it sounds. Husbands need to spend their day validating and accepting wife's feelings just like they spend time at work. Know how to empathize with your wife's pain, to feel her feelings and convey understanding. But the problem comes to marriage, when husbands want to solve wife's problems instead of understanding them. The problem is When she tells you about something and you passively listen until you have heard enough and then, as if to say I'm ready to move on to other things, you offer advice. You lecture instead of listen.

Husbands please make every effort of self-control to master bite your tongue and actively listen. **It is vital for the male man to consider this important fact.** Husbands say wives talk too much. Ladies, the next time your husband complains you talk too much, silence him with science. Tell him at length, of course it is all because of the Foxp2 protein.

It has been claimed previously that women speak about 20,000 words a day - some 13,000 more than the average man and scientists say a higher amount of the Foxp2 protein is the reason females are chattier. But now scientists have found the key to explaining why women are the more talkative gender. A study suggests that higher levels of the protein are found in the female brain.

Females like to match experiences, to draw one another out, to blitz in conversations. But when it comes to talking to their husbands, many wives feel like, talking to a husband is like being in a game alone.

To meet your wife's important need **to be known**, you need to actively listen to her, reflecting back to her what she is saying and feeling, and genuinely wanting to understand her. This point cannot be overemphasized. Females *need to have their feelings validated and accepted.* They need to have you see and experience the world the way they do, instead of explaining to them why they shouldn't see it that way.

Males have a tough time realizing that offering a listening ear is all a woman needs at times —or a comforting hug, a loving statement like "You are hurting, aren't you?" or "You are under a lot of pressure, aren't you?" Listening to your wife talk without offering quick solutions, is the only way to meet her need to be known. A Wife Needs to be Respected. Male men are usually quite unaware of how much female men need to be respected. Why? Because when male men are not respected they react very differently. A male man who does not feel respected, for example, is apt to become self-righteous and indignant. He feels even more worthy of respect when others don't respect him. He may even give less until he gets what he feels he deserves.

Female men operate differently. When they are not respected they feel insecure and lose their sense of self. That is why it is so vital for you to take exceptional care of your partner's need for respect. There are a number of ways to show respect to your wife. To begin with, do not try to change or manipulate her, but rather, honor her needs, wishes, values, and rights. I know a woman who, because of her upbringing, valued the tradition of having her door opened for her by her husband. She knew the custom was old-fashioned, but it meant a lot to her. For that reason, she asked her husband to do it. Her husband never took her request seriously. "You're kidding, right?" he'd say. "Nobody does that anymore. That's the reason why we've got power locks on the car." This husband laughed off his wife's request and weakened his opportunity to meet one of his wife's deepest needs —to be respected.

Respecting your wife also means including her in decisions. I am always amazed when I find a husband who wields or exerts all the power in a marriage. He makes all the decisions, regardless of what his wife thinks. I know of men who make decisions about spending on themselves their wives' resources without consulting them. A wife will make all the effort of buying a piece of land, plant fruit plants and vegetables, buy dairy cows and the husbands decides to squander it all . There isn't a quicker way to tear down a woman's sense of self and ruin the possibility of a happy marriage.

Husband develop and boost your wife's self-esteem and sense of security by asking her for her input whenever you may do, even on the trivial things. When you think of making a decision that might affect her, say: "I'm thinking about. What do you think of that?" or "I'm thinking we should. What would you like?"

Support and accept Your Wife. Respect says, I support you. You are valuable to me. You don't have to be any different from who you are.

In return for this respect, a wife will be able to relax. She will not have a compulsive need to prove herself as an equal but will automatically feel and be equal. What a wonderful way to live with a wife!

We believe that you now have a balanced perspective on God's order and purpose for marriage and have been prepared to challenge both the cultural and ecclesiastical norms and are have been equipped to confront them with raw biblical truth.

www.ingramcontent.com/pod-product-compliance
Lightning Source LLC
Chambersburg PA
CBHW060354080526
44583CB00012B/315